To Mom and Dad:
lovers of books, and
the power of words

WILLY NILLY

BILL CLINTON
SPEAKS OUT

Edward P. Moser

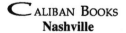
CALIBAN BOOKS
Nashville

Library of Congress Catalog Card Number:
94-070043

ISBN 1-879941-25-2

Published by Caliban Books
an imprint of J. S. Sanders & Company
Nashville, Tennessee

This book is a joint publication of Caliban Books and Adroit Press.

For special sales and premium opportunities write to:
Caliban Books
P.O. Box 50331
Nashville, Tennessee 37205

Caliban Books, March 1994 Edition
Manufactured in the United States of America

Cover design by Mike Stromberg

Cover photographs: Rueters/Bettmann

CONTENTS

Willy Nilly

ACKNOWLEDGMENTS

THIS BOOK WAS AIDED by the generous help of the staffs of the Library of Congress, the Alexandria and Arlington, Virginia public libraries, the Georgetown University press office, the Clinton White House documents room, the Clinton White House press office, the Bush Quayle '92 General Committee, and various offices and committees of the U.S. Congress. Most material was derived from news articles in *The Washington Post, The Washington Times, The Arkansas Democrat-Gazette* (formerly the *Arkansas Gazette*), and *The New York Times*. Articles by the White House reporters for *The Washington Post* and *The Washington Times*—particularly the syndicated columns of the *Times*—were especially useful.

A good summary of the Clinton/Gore campaign promises was found in *Putting People First* (Times Books/Random House, New York, 1992). In addition, a fine, objectively written short biography of Bill Clinton, *The Comeback Kid,* (Birch Lane Press/Carol Publishing Group, New York, 1992), by Charles F. Allen and Jonathan Portis, shed additional light on the object of attention.

Special thanks to Maryanne and Donna, Fran and Harry, Dean, Rita and Herb, Sonia, Gam, Larry, Mike M., Mike P., and Paul Ryan for their support and encouragement. Special thanks also to Mark Arey. And a word of gratitude to the fine people at Caliban, who don't know the meaning of the term "red tape."

INTRODUCTION

*"The President must articulate a vision
of where we're going."*
Bill Clinton

"We are, I think, in a crisis of meaning."
Hillary Rodham Clinton

THROUGHOUT HIS CAREER, Bill Clinton has shown a remarkable ability to take both sides of any topic, from the most critical to the very trivial. Some have characterized this behavior as indecision, or pandering to a fickle public, or worse. We prefer to give our President the benefit of the doubt, and ascribe his shifting stands to youthful inexperience.

This book is intended as a guide to help President Clinton, his associates, and the interested public make up their minds on the issues facing America. The book has a collection of Clinton's different positions as they have changed over time. It presents the issues in alphabetical order, with varying or contradictory statements, writings, or actions by Clinton or his staff listed under each issue heading. The book also provides the date of the statement or action.

Because Bill Clinton often changes his mind in the middle of a sentence, we've taken the liberty of splitting up contradictory sentences into their separate, coherent parts.

By way of illustration, we provide the following well-known passage from the book's section, "Marijuana, Smoking":

(July 23, 1991) "[I've never] broken any drug law."

(March 29, 1992) "I've never broken a state law."

(Next sentence) "But when I was in England I experimented with marijuana a time or two,"

(Same sentence) and I didn't like it. I didn't inhale it, and never tried it again."

Like Bill Clinton himself, *Willy Nilly* is aimed at multiple audiences. The lay reader without a specialized knowledge of politics can use the book to educate himself about the pressing issues of the day, as well as the details of the Clinton presidency. Administration officials, or those hoping to get a job with the White House, can use it to peer inside the complex mind of the Chief Executive. But the book is especially targeted at Bill Clinton himself.

By giving the man from Hope (and Hot Springs) a means of reviewing his own wayward record, it could assist him in finally taking a clear stand on something. The true purpose of this book, therefore, is not at all critical, but purely patriotic, and entirely constructive in nature.

Bill Clinton and Friends on the Issues

*All quotations are by Bill Clinton,
unless otherwise noted.*

A

Abortion

September 26, 1986: "I am opposed to abortion and to government funding of abortion."

June 1992: "Bill Clinton has always been pro-choice . . . Bill Clinton also supports the repeal of the Hyde Amendment, which prohibits federal funding for abortion in almost all situations."
Issue Brief, Bill Clinton for President Committee

September 1992: ". . . we will support the Freedom of Choice Act [permitting federal funding of abortions]"

Next phrase "not because we are pro-abortion, but because we think certain choices are too personal for politics."

Abortion, Parental Consent for

1990: ". . . I have also supported restrictions on public funding and a parental notification requirement for minors . . ."

September 1992: "[We] oppose . . . mandatory waiting periods or parental or spousal consent requirements [for abortions]. . ."

Abortion, Vice-President's Views on

May 26, 1987, from letter of then-Senator Gore to home-state residents: "During my 11 years in Congress, I have consistently opposed federal funding of abortions. In my opinion, it is wrong to spend federal funds for what is arguably the taking of a human life. Let me assure you that I share your belief that innocent human life must be protected, and I am committed to furthering this goal."

September 1992: "[We] oppose any federal attempt to limit access to abortion . . ."
Al Gore and Bill Clinton

Art, Prohibitions on Federally Funded

July 1992, on restrictions for projects funded by the National Endowment for the Arts: "I'm against it."

April 6, 1993, on law permitting content restrictions on Endowment-financed art: "Congress passed the law, and it's our job to uphold it."
Justice Department spokesman Mark Sakaley

AT&T, Breakup of

April 13, 1983: ". . . one of the worst ideas ever to be approved by our federal government."

July 26, 1992: "I think it worked in a number of ways. It lowered the cost of long-distance service. And it allowed a lot of people to get in and compete . . . [B]y and large, I think it was successful."

          ex   ex   ex

B

Baird, Zoe, Withdrawal of Attorney General Nomination for

January 1993: [A controversy erupted over reports that Zoe Baird, Bill Clinton's nominee for Attorney General, had employed illegal immigrants as her babysitter and part-time driver, and had failed to pay Social Security taxes on them.]

January 14, 1993: "It was fully disclosed. He [Bill Clinton] considered it [the tax and illegal alien issues] and did not think it was a problem."
Spokeswoman Dee Dee Myers

January 21, 1993: "[Clinton did] not believe they [he and Zoe Baird] had a discussion about it, no."
Communications Director George Stephanopoulos

January 21, 1993: "Mr. Clinton still believes she would make a fine Attorney General."
Communications Director George Stephanopoulos

Next morning: "With sadness, I accept your [Zoe Baird's] request that the nomination be withdrawn."

Balanced Budget

June 4, 1992: "[I] would present a five-year plan to balance the budget."

August 21, 1992: "My plan will . . . cut the deficit in half within four years."

August 5, 1993: ". . . finally they've [members of Congress] got somebody here who is serious about responsible budgeting instead of just talking about it."

Balanced Budget in Arkansas

August 21, 1992: "I have balanced 11 budgets in a row. . ."

1979-80, and 1983-1992: [Throughout Governor Clinton's terms of office, the Arkansas constitution had a balanced budget amendment, which mandates that state officials produce an annual balanced budget.]

Bosnia

August 5, 1992: "We may have to use military force. I would begin with air power . . . to try to restore the basic conditions of humanity."

March 28, 1993: "That really is a problem from hell. And I think that the United States is doing all we can to try to deal with that problem."
Secretary of State Warren Christopher

April 16, 1993: "I wouldn't rule out other steps; I wouldn't rule them in."

April 23, 1993: "The United States is not, should not, become involved as a partisan in a war."

Same day: "I think we should act. We should lead."

Same day: ". . . we must have a clearly defined objective . . ."

April 29, 1993: ". . . we think it's important that the United States fix its position and then talk to our allies about it."
    Secretary of State Warren Christopher

May 13, 1993: "So I can't give you a yes [on deployment of U.S. troops] right now; the thing is in flux."

Same interview: "I wouldn't rule out any option."

May 14, 1993: "We are not vacillating. We have a clear, strong policy."

June 15, 1993: "Our allies decided that they weren't prepared to go that far [with military intervention] at this time . . . I didn't change my mind."

June 17, 1993: ". . . my preference was for a multi-ethnic state in Bosnia. But if the parties themselves, including the Bosnian government . . . genuinely and honestly agree to a different solution [partitioning the country], then the United States would have to look at it very seriously."

Early in July 1993: "If the Serbs and the Croats persist in dismembering Bosnia through changes of borders by force or ethnic cleansing, they will place themselves beyond the pale of the international community . . . Stronger measures are not excluded."

July 21, 1993: "The United States is doing all it can consistent with our national interest."
    Secretary of State Warren Christopher

July 28, 1993: "The United States is committed to come to the aid of U.N. forces if they are attacked, and they have been."

Same day: ". . . we should continue to discuss a peaceful resolution of this."

August 6, 1993: "I would say to the Serbs they would be very unwise to depend on any indecision . . . We simply cannot accept empty promises as a cover for continued aggression."
Secretary of State Warren Christopher

September 2, 1993: ". . . I would remind you that the NATO military option is very much alive."

September 8, 1993: "As all of you know, anything we do has to have the support of Congress."

October 18, 1993: "The sharp escalation of shelling . . . may indicate a new attitude on the part of the Bosnian Serbs . . . that would have grave consequences."
State Department spokesman Michael McCurry

November 1993: "Is Bosnia horrifying, troubling? It is no more horrifying or troubling than the instances around this globe where populations, because of civil strife . . . face these kind of humanitarian disasters."
State Department spokesman Michael McCurry

January 11, 1994: "Air power might well be used . . ."

Same remarks: "[but only] if we were prepared to follow through, on the theory that we should not say things that we do not intend to do."

Bosnia, Effect of Bombing in

May 13, 1993: ". . . there is very little historical evidence that the use of air power alone produces results on the battlefield . . ."

Same interview, next response: "There's a lot to commend the arguments made by those who believe that air power will work . . ."

Bosnia, "Ethnic Cleansing" in

February 10, 1993: "Serbian ethnic cleansing has been pursued through mass murders, systematic beatings, and the rapes of Muslims and others, prolonged shellings of innocents in Sarajevo and elsewhere, forced displacement of entire villages, inhumane treatment of prisoners in detention camps . . . [it] tests what wisdom we have gathered from this bloody century."
Secretary of State Warren Christopher

March 28, 1993: "Let me put that situation in Bosnia in just a little broader framework. It's really a tragic problem. The hatred between all three groups—the Bosnians and the Serbs and the Croatians—is almost unbelievable. It's almost terrifying, and it's centuries old . . . The United States simply doesn't have the means to make people in that region of the world like each other."
Secretary of State Warren Christopher

August 1993: [The following State Department officials were among those who resigned over Bill Clinton's Bosnian policy:

- Marshall Freeman Harris, desk officer on Bosnia
- Jon Western, war crimes specialist
- Stephen Walker, desk officer on Croatia]

BTU Tax (Energy Tax)

February 17, 1993: "I recommend that we adopt a BTU tax on the heat content of energy . . ."

June 8, 1993: "It will not be a BTU tax."
Treasury Secretary Lloyd Bentsen

Same day: "We'll just see what comes out of it [Senate debate on the issue]."

July 18, 1993: ". . . I think the likelihood is that we're looking more at a gas tax than a BTU tax."
Budget Director Leon Panetta

BTU Tax, Reaction to Reversal of Position on

[In the spring of 1993, Bill Clinton withdrew support for a BTU tax after he had pushed for its passage by the House of Representatives. This displeased some House Democrats who had taken the political risk of supporting a tax increase.]

June 10, 1993: ". . . we were going to censure those that walked away from the President, and now it's reported that the President walked away from us."
Democratic Congressman Charles Rangel

" . . . we've been left hanging out on the plank . . ."
Democratic Congresswoman Patricia Schroeder

&a.   &a.   &a.

C

Campaign Finance Reform

May 7, 1993: "First the plan will impose strict"

Next phrase: "but voluntary campaign limits on spending in congressional campaigns . . ."

Catholic Church

January 1992, at pro-abortion rally: "The first 400 years black people had their freedom aborted, and the church said nothing . . . Look at who is fighting the pro-choice movement: a celibate, male-dominated church . . . We would like for the right-to-life, anti-choice groups to really get over their love affair with the fetus, and start supporting the children."
    Joycelyn Elders, later Bill Clinton's Surgeon General

September 11, 1992, in speech at University of Notre Dame:" . . . I enrolled at Georgetown University, the nation's oldest Jesuit college . . . I loved the Catholic understanding of history and tradition and how they shape us."

Children, Government Role in Raising

July 16, 1992: "[G]overnments don't raise children; parents do."

September 1992: "Create a nationwide program . . . to provide health-care services to more low-income women and their children . . . Develop a comprehensive maternal and child health network . . . Fully fund the Women, Infants and Children (WIC) program . . ."

February 15, 1991: "A lot of programs . . . basically put too much responsibility on the mother. I mean, if the mother knew what she was supposed to do, she would go do it."
Hillary Rodham Clinton

China, Sending Envoys to

October 1, 1992: "President Bush's ambivalence about supporting democracy, his eagerness to befriend potentates and dictators has shown itself again and again. It has been a disservice . . . to our democratic values . . ."

October 11, 1992, in criticizing the previous Administration's China policy: "Mr. Bush sent two people in secret to toast the Chinese leaders and basically tell them not to worry about it [suppression of political dissent]."

October 20, 1993: "You cannot preach and criticize from 7,000 miles away. You have to engage on a more personal level, and that is why Clinton is trying to send cabinet members over here [China] to discuss these difficulties . . ."
Agriculture Secretary Mike Espy

Civil Rights, Setting Personal Example for

October 3, 1991: "[Our opponents] want us to look at each other across a racial divide . . ."

[Top White House officials who, into 1992-1993, played golf at a racially segregated country club:

- Bill Clinton
- Chief of Staff Thomas "Mack" McLarty
- Associate Attorney General Webster Hubbell
- Associate White House Counsel William Kennedy]

July 16, 1992: "... [we] must now accept the obligation of proving that freedom from prejudice is the heart and soul of community, that yes, we can get along ..."
    Al Gore

Civil Rights Laws in Arkansas and the United States

[During Governor Clinton's terms of office (1979–1980 and 1983–1992), Arkansas remained one of only two states without a law that banned job discrimination, and one of only nine states without a law that forbade housing discrimination.]

September 1992: "Support strong and effective enforcement of the 1991 Civil Rights Act ..."

Clinton, Bill, Foreign Leaders' Praise for

February 14, 1993: "There are some trying to portray the anti-war past of Clinton as a matter of personal weakness, while we consider such a stand as a mark of strength."
    Iraqi President Saddam Hussein

March 3, 1993: "Actually, in Clinton's program I see elements I like a lot."
    Former Polish Communist dictator Gen. Wojciech Jarulzelski

July 1993: "[Clinton is] a decent man, a man of peace. It seems to me that he is of a different generation of North Americans."
    Cuban despot Fidel Castro

Summer 1993: "Clinton and I belong to the same democratic camp ... [He is a] kind, well-intentioned man ... [But he] must resist the temptation to demonstrate that he is decisive."
    Libyan dictator Col. Moammar Gadhafi

Clinton, Bill, Friends of Bill on

February 1992: "I hope he's telling the truth, but I've got some doubts."
Democratic Senator Bob Kerrey

March 6, 1992: "[S]ome people will say anything to be elected President."
Paul Tsongas, former Democratic Senator and Presidential candidate

Same day: "Bill Clinton is a pander bear."
Paul Tsongas

January 1993: "[T]he clatter of campaign promises being tossed out the window."
Democratic Senator Daniel Patrick Moynihan

May 1993: ". . . like Bill Clinton, going in a thousand different directions . . ."
Democratic Congressman Joe Kennedy

May 1993: "[he] feels like a mosquito in a nudist colony. You know, there's so much territory to cover, you don't know where to land first."
Clinton consultant Paul Begala

June 1993: "I'm trying to play by the rules. They keep changing them."
Lani Guinier, withdrawn White House nominee for Assistant Attorney General for Civil Rights

June 1993: ". . . the back-and-forth, up-and-down, in-and-out motion of this administration and of this president."
Democratic Congressman Kweisi Mfume

July, 1993: "How do I say this politely? This Administration is overconfident in the capacity to charm, talk, and persuade, and underappreciates the value of ideas and strong committments."
Paul Tsongas

Clinton, Bill, White House Counselor David Gergen on

May 13, 1993: "[Clinton] has gone from poor to perilous.He's not only gone off track, he's going around in circles."

May 30, 1993, after Gergen's appointment as Presidential Counselor: "[Clinton's] accomplished a lot. He's had good, strong leadership . . ."

Clinton, Bill, Former Surgeon General C. Everett Koop and

September 22, 1993: "Now, nobody has to take my word for this [reputed savings from health care plan]. You can ask Dr. Koop. He's up here with us tonight, and I thank him for being here."

November 1993: "I'm telling you what the problem is: He's [Bill Clinton's] trying to please everyone."
C. Everett Koop

Commerce Secretary, Foreign Lobbyists and the

August 21, 1992: "In a Clinton Administration, American trade negotiators will never forget that they're working for American business, American workers, and American taxpayers—and nobody else."

1982-86: [Ron Brown, later Bill Clinton's Secretary of Commerce, worked as a registered agent for the government of Haitian dictator Jean-Claude "Baby Doc" Duvalier.]

May 1993: [Ron Brown denied, through a spokesman, that he ever met Vietnamese businessman Nguyen Van Hao, who was alleged to have made payments to Brown in an effort to lift the U.S. trade

embargo on Vietnam.] "Mr. Brown has never had any contact with any of the people named, not Mr. Hao . . ."
Commerce Department spokesman Jim Desler

September 28, 1993, in admitting Ron Brown met the Vietnamese businessman: "The secretary assured him [President Clinton] that they [Brown and Hao] did not discuss money . . ."
Press Secretary Dee Dee Myers

Commercial Mining on Park Land in Arkansas

April 9, 1987: "Governor Bill Clinton has signed legislation allowing commercial diamond mining at the Crater of Diamonds State Park."
Arkansas Gazette

June 26, 1990: "I've never supported commercial mining."

Condom Ads

January 4, 1994: [Federally funded commercials supporting the use of condoms to prevent AIDS were broadcast in early 1994. One radio commercial featured Anthony Kiedis, singer for the rock band, The Red Hot Chili Peppers, and a convicted sex offender.] "I've been naked on stage. I've been naked on magazine covers . . . I might as well get naked again . . . What I have here is a condom, a latex condom. I wear one whenever I have sex . . . You can be naked without being exposed."
Anthony Kiedis

January 7, 1994, as the Clinton Administration withdrew the ad: "We do not feel he is an appropriate spokesperson."
Director of the federal Centers
for Disease Control and Prevention David Satcher

Credibility, Statements on

January 9, 1992: "I'm Bill Clinton, and I believe you deserve more than 30-second ads or vague promises."

May 21, 1992: "A president's words can move a nation, but talk must be backed up with action or we risk diminishing the bully pulpit into a pulpit of bull."

August 21, 1992: "No wonder Americans hate politics, when year in, year out, they hear politicians make promises that won't come true because they don't even mean them."

June 17, 1993: ". . . the most important thing is that we attempt, you and I, to create an atmosphere of trust and respect . . . I'm going to do my best to be honest with you . . ."

December 22, 1993: "A lesson I've learned as president: words are deeds in a fundamental way."

Cuomo, Mario

January 27, 1992: [Gennifer Flowers released a tape, dating from September 1991, which contained the following remarks:]

Clinton: "Boy, he [Cuomo] is so aggressive."

Flowers: "I wouldn't be surprised if he didn't have some Mafioso major connections."

Clinton: "Well, he acts like one. [Laughs.]"

January 28, 1992: "[I] meant simply to imply that Governor Cuomo is a tough and worthy competitor."

Same response: "If the remarks on the tape left anyone with the impression that I was disrespectful to either Governor Cuomo or Italian-Americans, then I deeply regret it."

June 16, 1992: "I think Governor Cuomo would be a good Supreme Court Justice . . ."

D

Day Person vs. Night Person

1993: "A little of both. That's the problem."

Death Penalty Law, Credit Claimed for Passing

March 1990: "Governor Clinton has passed legislation demanding the death penalty for dealers who kill with drugs."
  Clinton campaign ad

April 8, 1990: ". . . legislation that specifically called for the death penalty for drug kingpins failed in a state Senate Judiciary Committee . . ."
  Arkansas Gazette

Decisiveness

January 14, 1993: "The American people would think I was foolish if I said, 'I will not respond to changing circumstances.'"

June 15, 1993: "There is no wavering . . . this is the most decisive presidency you've had in a very long time on all the big issues that matter."

Fall 1993, on opinion polls showing the public in a pessimistic mood: "I think in a way it may be my fault . . . I go from one thing to another."

Defense Cuts and Deficit Reduction

September 1992: "The funds we save will be spent on rebuilding America and reducing our deficit."

Same document: "As we cut our defense budget, we must transfer the savings, dollar for dollar, into investment in the American economy . . ."

Deficit, Estimating the

June 23, 1992: "When I began the campaign, the projected deficit was $250 billion. Now it's up to $400 billion."

February 15, 1993: ". . . I can't [avoid a tax increase] because the deficit has increased so much beyond my earlier estimates . . ."

February 17, 1993: [The size of the 1993 deficit, according to the Clinton budget proposal was $258.2 billion]

Deficit, Reducing the Size of the

September 1992: "Never again should we pass on our debts to our children while their futures silently slip through our fingers."

August 6, 1993: [The projected increase in the national debt, or accumulated deficits, according to the budget plan enacted by Bill Clinton and Congress:]

1994	1995	1996	1997	1998
$3.5 trillion	$3.8 trillion	$4.1 trillion	$4.4 trillion	$4.7 trillion

"Deficit Reduction" Accord, Follow-up to

August 2, 1993: "We're just getting started on the spending reductions."

August-November 1993: [In the four months following the August 1993 "deficit reduction" budget, Bill Clinton approved or proposed the following programs:

- $350 billion in new health care subsidies
- $16 billion in additional health care subsidies for small businesses and low-income workers
- Greater federal share in paying for disaster relief, from 75 percent to 90 percent
- Large share of $8 billion fund for Mexico's environment
- $3.9 billion in greater spending on unemployment
- $3 billion in loan guarantees to the shipbuilding industry]

Demonstrations, Organizing Anti-Vietnam-War

December 3, 1969: "I went to Washington to work in the national headquarters of the [anti-war] Moratorium, then to England to organize the Americans here [in London] for demonstrations Oct. 15 and Nov. 16."
Letter to Director of University of Arkansas Reserve Officer Training Corps (ROTC) program

February 15, 1988: "The stories you mentioned . . . about Governor Clinton participating in anti-military demonstrations in the late 1960s or early 1970s are purely invention with no basis in fact."
Clinton Press Secretary Mike Gauldin

September 1992: "He [Clinton] was one of the main organizers [in England] of the American Embassy protest in 1969."
Rev. Richard McSorley, friend of Bill Clinton

Demonstrators, Meeting Overseas with Anti-Vietnam-War

October 7, 1992:

Question: "So this Oslo visit [to Norway in 1969] . . . was a social visit that didn't necessarily have to do with [the] peace [movement]?"
    TV host Phil Donahue

Answer: "No, it didn't have anything to do [with the peace movement]—I was going through Norway . . . We [myself and friend Rev. Richard McSorley] went to the university together. I said hello to the people he was meeting, and then I went to meet the guy I was meeting."

October 6, 1992: "We went to various places and he [Clinton] went with me, and he participated in all the [anti-war] discussions [over nine hours] . . . There were conscientious objectors we visited . . . I don't recall it [Clinton going to meet a friend]. I think he was with me the whole day."
    Rev. Richard McSorley, friend of Bill Clinton

"Diversity"

October 19, 1992: ". . . I owe the American people . . . a Cabinet and appointments that look like America . . ."

January 1993: [13 of the first 18 Cabinet selections in the Clinton Administration were lawyers.]

January-June 1993: [Some of the high-ranking people selected by Clinton who were millionaires:

- Deputy Treasury Secretary Robert Altman
- Interior Secretary Bruce Babbitt
- Treasury Secretary Lloyd Bentsen
- Commerce Secretary Ron Brown

- Secretary of State Warren Christopher
- Supreme Court Justice Ruth Bader Ginsburg
- Energy Secretary Hazel O'Leary
- Labor Secretary Robert Reich
- Education Secretary Richard Riley
- Director of National Economic Council Robert Rubin]

Draft, Evading the Vietnam

December 3, 1969, letter to director of University of Arkansas ROTC program: "First, I want to thank you, not just for saving me from the draft . . ."

1979: "I put myself in a position to be drafted. Not very many people were doing that . . . the draft was the law and if I'd been called, I was ready to go and do the best I could."

October 23, 1991: "We must make good on the words of Thomas Jefferson, who said, 'A debt of service is due from every man to his country . . . '"

September 1992: "I didn't go back through all my letters, notes, to put this all back together again because the issue has been raised on me before in Arkansas. And when it had, everybody told me I hadn't done anything wrong."

September 15, 1992: "[T]here is concern that it could take a political toll if the public thought he were afraid to face the issue."
Campaign spokeswoman Dee Dee Myers

October 6, 1992: "You drew a conclusion that I had somehow tried to have it both ways in the Vietnam war. That's a load of bull. I was opposed to it. I was on record opposed to it early on. I never denied it."

Draft Evasion and the Arkansas Senator

December 1991: "I am positive I never asked anyone [on the staff of then-Arkansas Senator William Fulbright] for that [help in avoiding the draft]. No. Never."

September 16, 1992: "Governor Clinton has no specific recollection of any specific actions [in discussing his draft status with Fulbright's staff]."
Clinton aide Betsey Wright

September 18, 1992: "[Governor Clinton] talked to the Fulbright people about what his options were . . ."
Campaign spokeswoman Dee Dee Myers

Draft Evasion and Family Influence

September 1, 1992: [Bill Clinton had the following response about a report that Clinton's uncle tried to get him a Naval Reserve slot as a substitute for the draft:] "It's all news to me."

September 4, 1992: "I did not know of any efforts to secure a Naval Reserve assignment before [the head of the local draft board] mentioned it to me [in March] . . ."

September 19, 1992: "He [Clinton] never asked for special treatment."
Campaign spokeswoman Dee Dee Myers

October 6, 1992: "Since he's running for President he can't afford to be clear on any of these things [about his draft history] . . . He'd be foolish to tell the truth about it. He doesn't have to lie; he just doesn't say what happened."
Rev. Richard McSorley, friend of Bill Clinton

October 19, 1992: "If I had it [the draft] to do over again, I might answer the questions a little better."

Draft Evasion and the ROTC Letter

December 3, 1969, letter from Bill Clinton to director of University of Arkansas ROTC program: "I am so sorry to be so long in writing."

Next sentence: "I know I promised to let you hear from me at least once a month, and from now on you will . . ."

Same letter: ". . . I began to think I had deceived you, not by lies—there were none—but by failing to tell you all the things I'm writing now . . ."

Same letter: "[On] Sept. 12 I stayed up all night writing a letter to the chairman of my draft board . . . stating that I couldn't do the ROTC after all and would he please draft me as soon as possible."

Next sentence: "I never mailed the letter,"

Next phrase: "but I did carry it on me every day until I got on the plane to return to England . . ."

Draft Notice, Receipt of a

December 1991: ". . . I told the [draft board] I expected to be called [i.e., sent a draft notice] while I was over there [at Oxford] the first year, but they never did [send a draft notice]."

August 25, 1992, before the veterans organization, the American Legion: "In 1969, while studying at Oxford, I received a draft notice"

Next phrase: "which arrived late."

Drug Treatment Programs

July 1, 1993: "Our aim is to cut off the demand for drugs at the knees through prevention. That means more and better education, more treatment, more rehabilitation."

Same day: [The House of Representatives cut $231 million from Clinton's proposed budget for drug education and treatment.] "Frankly, the administration supported the reductions, informally. They told us this would make a pretty good place to start [making budget reductions]."
Member of congressional staff, as reported by *The Washington Post*

Same day: "That's something [reputed Administration support for drug program cuts] that's being investigated. Everybody in the Administration is trying to figure out what's going on."
White House drug policy office spokeswoman Adrienne O'Neal

July 7, 1993: "Certainly, it's [the cutbacks] not what we wanted to see happen."
Head of Clinton drug policy office Lee Brown

Drugs, Legalizing

October 11, 1992: ". . . I have a brother who's a recovering drug addict. . . . I can tell you this. If drugs were legal, I don't think he'd be alive today. I am adamantly opposed to legalizing drugs."

December 7, 1993: "And I do feel that we would markedly reduce our crime rate if drugs were legalized."
Surgeon General Joycelyn Elders

Same day: "She [Elders] is not speaking for the Administration on this issue. "
Press Secretary Dee Dee Myers

[On December 20, 1993, Kevin Elders, son of Surgeon General Joycelyn Elders, was arrested and charged with selling cocaine to an undercover police officer in a public park.]

Drugs, War on

July 16, 1992: "[My opponent has] talked a lot about drugs, but he hasn't helped people on the front line to wage that war on drugs and crime, but I will."

June 19, 1993: "I would hope that we would provide them [prostitutes] Norplant, so they could still use sex if they must to buy their drugs and not have unplanned babies."
  Joycelyn Elders, Surgeon General

E

Education Spending under George Bush

February 26, 1990: [Then-Governor Clinton defended the Bush
Administration against charges
that it was not giving Arkansas
enough funds for its schools:]
"[The charges] are not accurate
. . . not fair."

September 1992: "For four
years we've heard a lot of talk
about the 'Education President'
but seen little government action to invest in the collective talents
of our people."

Elderly, Views on Earnings of the

September 1992: "Lift the Social Security earnings test limitation
[cap on benefits based on a person's income] so that older
Americans are able to help rebuild our economy . . ."

August 1993: [The budget passed by Bill Clinton and Congress
taxed up to 85 percent of the Social Security benefits of
individuals earning more than $34,000 a year.]

Environment, Foreign Aid and the

October 13, 1992: [The following exchange took place between
Dan Quayle and Al Gore during the vice-presidential debate:]

Quayle: ". . . one of the proposals that Senator Gore has suggested is to have the taxpayers of America spend $100 billion a year on environmental projects in foreign countries—"

Gore: "That's not true."

Quayle: ". . . well, Senator, it's in your book [*Earth in the Balance*]. On page 304."

Gore: "No, it's not."

[In 1992, Al Gore recommended just such a foreign aid fund which he called a "Global Marshall Plan:"] ". . . the annual U.S. expenditures for the Marshall Plan [for Europe] between 1948 and 1951 were close to 2 percent of our GNP [gross national product]. A similar percentage today [for an 'environmental Marshall Plan'] would be almost $100 billion a year . . ."

Al Gore, *Earth in the Balance,* p. 304

Environment: Gore Family and the Garbage Dump

July 16, 1992: "The task of saving the Earth's environment must and will become the central organizing principle of the post-Cold War world."
Al Gore

1992: "Our [family] farm taught me a lot about how nature works."
Al Gore

October 1992: [A news report stated that an open trash dump, with pesticide cans, old tires, and bags of trash, was on the property of Albert Gore Sr., the father of Al Gore, in the estate that adjoins his son's house.]

October 28, 1992: "It [the dump] may be ugly, but there is nothing illegal about it."
Marla Romash, spokeswoman for Al Gore

Environmental Record

1992: "To many Arkansas environmentalists, Clinton has a record of poor appointments . . .
Not until the contamination
[of a nearby creek with
poultry wastes] had
reached crisis levels did the
Governor intervene . . .
Local environmentalists are
dismayed with Clinton's inaction concerning the permission and construction of medical and hazardous waste incinerators."
League of Conservation Voters

September 1992: "Governor Clinton has also helped Arkansas live up to its nickname—the Natural State. It has some of the cleanest water and purest air in the nation, and Bill Clinton is part of the reason why."
Clinton/Gore campaign document

Europe and Japan, Importance to the United States of

February 12, 1993, in meeting with Japan's Foreign Minister:"[Japan is] the most important partner of the United States."
Secretary of State Warren Christopher

January 9, 1994, in meeting with European leaders: "And you [Europe] remain our most valued partner . . ."

Executive Salaries

January 1992: "In 11 years as governor, I've never had a pay raise."

1979-80, and 1983-1992: [Throughout Governor Clinton's terms of office the Arkansas state constitution fixed the salary of the governor.]

Extramarital Affairs, Allegations by Arkansas State Troopers Concerning

December 19, 1993: "[The charges are] ridiculous . . . [with] nothing that dignifies a further response."
White House senior aide Bruce Lindsey

December 22, 1993, Presidential Press Conference: "We did not do anything wrong."

Same Press Conference: "So none of this ever happened?"
Peter Maer, White House Correspondent for Mutual and NBC Radio News

Reply: "I have nothing else to say. . . . We . . . we did, if, the, the, I, I, the stories are just as they have been said. They're outrageous and they're not so . . . We have not done anything wrong. The allegations on abuse of the state or the positions I have—they're just not true."

February 3, 1994: [In a speech to an audience at the District of Columbia's Kramer Junior High School, in response to questioning about family values and the high incidence of teenage pregnancy, Bill Clinton advised:] "[Sex] is not a sport: this is a solemn responsibility."

ૐ   ૐ   ૐ

F

Farm Research, Reducing Bloat in

February 17, 1993: [A Clinton Administration book detailing its budget proposals listed the following cuts, in millions of dollars, to "Eliminate Agricultural Research Service earmarked facilities construction."]

1993	1994	1995	1996	1997	1998
—	-1	-6	-7	-10	-10

Same day: [The same document listed the following budget increases, in millions of dollars, for "Agricultural Research Service: Enhanced facility maintenance":]

1993	1994
30	8

First Hundred Days

June 23, 1992: "I'll have the [economic] bills ready the day after I'm inaugurated . . . we'll have a hundred-day period . . . It will be the most productive in modern history."

November 16, 1992, 13 days after the election: "I do think we'll be able to do some things within a hundred days. . . ."

January 11, 1993: "People of the press are expecting [us] to have some 100-day program. We never ever had one."
Spokeswoman Dee Dee Myers

January 14, 1993: "I don't know who led you to believe that [I would impose a swift introduction of economic legislation], but I'm the only one who's authorized to talk about it."

May 10, 1993: ". . . I knew when I got there [the White House]it wasn't going to happen overnight."

First Lady's Accent

[On "60 Minutes" in January 1992:] "Her voice [Hillary Rodham Clinton's] carried the definite inflections of an Arkansas accent."

Next sentence: "This woman from a Chicago suburb who was educated at Wellesley and Yale had, until recently, spoken in the neutral tones of the Midwest."
From biography of Bill Clinton

July 11, 1993: "Oh well, we all have different roles that we play in our lives at different times."
Hillary Rodham Clinton

First Lady's Name

[In Arkansas before Bill Clinton's 1980 loss in the governor's race:] "Hillary Rodham Clinton."

[In Arkansas after loss of the governorship, and in subsequent, successful gubernatorial campaigns:] "Mrs. Hillary Clinton."

[During the Presidential campaign, before November 3, 1992, Election Day:] "Mrs. Hillary Clinton."

[After November 3, 1992:] "Hillary Rodham Clinton."

January 30, 1992, on deciding in the 1980s to be called "Mrs. Clinton" : "It was a personal decision,"

Next phrase: "but it was prompted by political considerations."
Hillary Rodham Clinton

May 29, 1992: "There is no dress rehearsal for life, and you will have to ad lib your way through every scene."
Hillary Rodham Clinton

Flowers, Gennifer

January 17, 1992, on press reports about Bill Clinton's alleged womanizing: ". . . they've been exposed as the trash they are."

January 26, 1992: "You know, I have acknowledged wrongdoing. I have acknowledged causing pain in my marriage . . ."

Foreign Intervention, Congressional Approval for Armed

September 8, 1993, on possible U.S. air strikes in Bosnia: "And of course for me to do it, the Congress would have to agree."

October 18, 1993, on possible deployment of U.S. troops in Haiti: "I thought I ought to say clearly today that I would strenuously oppose such attempts [by Congress] to encroach on the president's foreign policy powers."

Foster, Vincent, Office Search of Deceased White House Aide

[On July 20, 1993, White House Deputy Counsel Vincent Foster was found dead of a gunshot wound at Fort Marcy Park in Northern Virginia. Clinton Administration officials, led by White House Counsel Bernard Nussbaum, subsequently removed from Foster's office records pertaining to Whitewater Development Corp., a controversial Arkansas real estate venture partially owned by Bill and Hillary Rodham Clinton, and under investigation by federal authorities. Foster was Deputy White House Counsel, the Clintons' personal attorney on matters relating to Whitewater, and a former partner of Hillary Rodham Clinton in the Rose law firm in Little Rock.]

July 30, 1993: ". . . I think that Mr. Nussbaum conducted a very thorough investigation [of Foster's office], particularly in terms of what [investigators] were looking for. I mean, he went through the files and described what the issues were [to investigators] and what the contents of the files were . . ."
  Press Secretary Dee Dee Myers

December 20, 1993: "Following the death of Vincent Foster . . . those files that pertained to the personal legal affairs of the President and Mrs. Clinton including . . . Whitewater Development Corp . . . were [removed from the office and] sent to the Clintons' personal attorney."
  White House Communications Director Mark Gearan

Foster, Vincent, Status of Office Files of Deceased White House Aide

[In December, 1993, a number of Congressmen and newspapers demanded that Foster's records be turned over to a federal inquiry into the Whitewater real estate venture.]

December 21, 1993, in declining to release the files: "I think we've done what we should have done and don't feel the need to do any more than we've done."
  Hillary Rodham Clinton

December 23, 1993: "The President has instructed his personal attorney to provide . . . all documents relating to the Whitewater Development Corporation, including those in the files of Vincent Foster . . ."
  White House Communications Director Mark Gearan

G

Gasoline Tax

[During his 1979–80 term Governor Clinton signed large increases in Arkansas' gasoline tax and car title and registration fees.]

July 16, 1992: "[George Bush] has raised taxes on the people driving pickup trucks . . . We can do better."

June 10, 1993: "I haven't signed off yet on any [gasoline tax] proposal."

August 3, 1993: "The plan asks . . . a 4.3 cent a gallon increase in the gas tax."

Gays in the Military

September 1992: "[I will] issue executive orders to repeal the ban on gays and lesbians from military or foreign service."

November 16, 1992: ". . . I've made no decision on a timetable except that I want to firmly proceed . . ."

January 13, 1993: "I have not backed away from gays in the military."

March 24, 1993: "This is not an area where I have expertise. . . ."

May 10, 1993: "I hope my position will prevail. That's sort of my position."

May 14, 1993: "I support the present code of conduct . . ."

July 14, 1993: "My sense is there's still some difference of opinion even among the service chiefs about what they want, but I hope they'll come up with something that everyone can agree is fair and we can all live with. We'll just have to see."

October 26, 1993: ". . . the presence . . . of persons who engage in homosexual conduct or who, by their statements, demonstrate a propensity to engage in homosexual conduct, seriously impairs the accomplishment of the military mission."
Solicitor General Drew S. Days III

"Global Warming," Delay and Changes to Plan for Reducing

1992: "[Global warming is] the most serious crisis that we have ever faced."
Al Gore

July 16, 1992: "They embarrassed our nation when the whole world was asking for American leadership in confronting the environmental crisis."
Al Gore

[On April 21, 1993, Bill Clinton declared an August deadline for setting specific steps to reduce pollution which he said contributes to global warming.]

August 15, 1993, upon missing self-imposed deadline for action: "The delay speaks to a strong feeling that additional time would produce an additional product."
White House spokeswoman Marla Romash

[On October 19, 1993, Bill Clinton and Al Gore announced a plan based largely on suggested guidelines for industry, instead of specific, mandatory steps to reduce pollution relating to global warming:] "Voluntary is not a dirty word."
Energy Secretary Hazel O'Leary

Same day: "But the magnitude of the threat should galvanize, not paralyze, our response."
Clinton/Gore Plan

Golf Handicap

August 31, 1993: "Well, it's about a 14,"

Next phrase: "but I haven't played in a while, so it's probably closer to an 18 today,"

Next phrase: "and because I haven't had the time to play as much as I'd like I'm having trouble getting off the tee,"

Next phrase: "so my handicap probably doesn't mean a whole lot right now."

Government Role towards Private Industry

1992: "[I recommend] [t]ax incentives for the new technologies and disincentives for the old. . . . Research and development funding for new technologies and prospective bans on the old ones . . . The promise of large profits in a market certain to emerge as older technologies are phased out."
Al Gore

August 21, 1992: "I don't believe in government picking winners and losers [in the market economy]."

Government Workers, Decreasing the Number of

September 7, 1993: "This reduction in the [federal] work force will total 252,000 positions . . ."
Al Gore

October 13, 1993: "I do not know the origin of the 252,000 figure."

Lorraine Green, Deputy Director of the federal Office of Personnel Management

Guinier, Lani: Withdrawal of Nomination for Assistant Attorney General for Civil Rights

May 11, 1993: "I want to say a special word of support for Lani Guinier. I went to law school with her, and . . . she actually sued me once. Not only that, she didn't lose. And I nominated her anyway. So the Senate ought to be able to put up with a little controversy in the cause of civil rights and go on and confirm her."

May 14, 1993: "I would never have appointed anybody to public office if they had to agree with everything I believe in."

June 2, 1993: "I think that I have to talk to some of the Senators about it because of the reservations that have been raised."

Same response: ". . . I think any reasonable reading of her writings would lead someone to conclude that a lot of the attacks cannot be supported by a fair reading of the writings."

Next sentence: "And that's not to say I agree with everything in the writings. I don't."

June 3, 1993: "It is with deep regret that I am announcing tonight the withdrawal of the nomination of Lani Guinier . . . [Guinier's writings] do not represent the views that I expressed on civil rights during my campaign, and views that I hold very dearly"

Next phrase: "even though there is much in them with which I agree."

Two remarks later: "Now I want to make it clear that that is not to say that I agree with all the attacks on her. She has been subject to a vicious series of willful distortions on many issues."

That evening: "I love her [Lani Guinier]. I think she's wonderful."

Same evening: "If she called me and told me she needed $5,000, I'd take it from my account and send it to her, no questions asked. It was the hardest decision I've had to make since I became president."

Guinier, Lani: Followup Selection for Assistant Attorney General for Civil Rights

[In November 1993, John Payton, Bill Clinton's second choice for Assistant Attorney General for Civil Rights, was heavily criticized over his voting record. Although his job would place him in charge of enforcing the Voting Rights Act, Payton admitted that, from 1984 to 1988, he had not registered to vote.]

Fall 1993: "Well, it was a mistake not to vote. I wish I had voted. It's more than embarrassing. People did sacrifice to get that right."
John Payton, second choice for Assistant Attorney General for Civil Rights

November 4, 1993: "We are going forward with our leading contender [Payton]. Anybody who says to the contrary is wrong . . . [Officials doubting the nomination] are chicken. Let them go on the record. They're wrong. We are gathering support now."
Associate Attorney General Webster Hubbell

December 17, 1993, in the wake of lukewarm congressional support for the nomination: "Sadly, I am writing to request that you [Janet Reno] withdraw my name from consideration."
Nominee for Assistant Attorney General John Payton

Fall 1993: ". . . nobody's accused me of just running away from things. I haven't stiffed the civil-rights community or anything like that."

Gun Control

November 1, 1990: "I'm not for gun control."

Fall 1993, during interview: ". . . pass the Brady bill [for a waiting period on handguns] . . . Virginia's once-a-month handgun purchase limit is worth adopting . . . we need to look at this whole business of licensing federal gun dealers . . . there are certain kinds of guns that can be banned."

December 20, 1993: "You are going to see an increase in the licensing fees for the selling of guns."
    Treasury Secretary Lloyd Bentsen

ó&&   ó&&   ó&&

H

Haircut Costing $200
from Hollywood Hairdresser
on Runway of Los Angeles International (LAX)
Airport

May 20, 1993: "According to the
information I had, there was no hold
placed on the air traffic at LAX."

Same press conference: "It wouldn't
necessarily be unusual to have some sort
of delays."
Communications Director George
Stephanopoulos

Same day: "Bill Clinton has challenging
hair to say the least. Even on a good day
it sometimes looks like worn-out Brillo."
Clinton consultant Paul Begala

*May 24, 1993, in response to criticism
over "Hair Force One":* "We had a
good week last week."

Same day: "The president was
disappointed in the week."
Communications Director George
Stephanopoulos

May 27, 1993: "I'd never do that
[deliberately delay air passengers with a
haircut]. I wasn't raised that way."

Haiti, Remarks on Sending U.S. Troops to

September 27, 1993, during a speech at the U.N. referring to "peacekeeping" missions: "When lives are on the line, you cannot let the reach of the U.N. exceed its grasp."

October 11, 1993: [At the seaport of Haiti's capital, heavily armed thugs backed by Haiti's military prevented the planned landing of 193 lightly armed U.S. military personnel comprising part of a U.N. mission to train Haiti's military. The U.S. troops sailed home.]

October 14, 1993: ". . . I was not about to put 200 American Seabees into a potentially dangerous situation for which they were neither trained nor armed to deal with."

Same day: "[I must make] absolutely clear . . . [in] the most forceful terms . . . [that] no one in the international community . . . walk away [from Haiti]."

October 16, 1993: "We had every reason to think they'd [the U.S. troops] be well received, we thought there was going to be a greeting party."
   Secretary of State Warren Christopher

Haiti, Role of U.S. Troops Sent to

October 12, 1993: "I have no intention of asking our young people in uniform . . . to do anything other than implement a peace agreement."

Same day: "This is not peacekeeping. This is not peacemaking."

Haitian Refugees, Forcible Return of

March 3, 1992: "I think the President [George Bush] played racial politics with the Haitian refugees. I wouldn't be shipping those poor people back."

January 14, 1993: ". . . the practice of returning those who fled Haiti by boat will continue . . . Those who do leave Haiti . . . will be stopped and directly returned . . ."

Same day: "I still believe the policy should be changed."

Same day: "I still believe just exactly what I said, that everybody is entitled to a hearing who seeks to become a refugee in this country."

Same day: "Sometimes people only hear half the message."

October 14, 1993: ". . . when I took office, what we had was everybody in Haiti thinking about whether they could leave and come to the United States because they thought there was no way that anybody would ever stick up for the democratic process in Haiti."

"Head Start" Program for Pre-School Children

February 17, 1993: "We all know that Head Start . . . saves money . . . For every dollar we invest today, we'll save three tomorrow."

March 8, 1993: "The well-known formula cited by President Clinton ('one dollar spent now saves three later') reflects the success of one *non*-Head Start project . . . in the 1960s."
   Time magazine

Health Care Budget

November 20, 1991: "We could cover every American with the money we're [now] spending . . ."

January 26, 1993: ". . . [we'll need] $30 billion or $90 billion of additional annual expenditure by the government by 1997."
Top health care adviser Ira Magaziner

April 20, 1993: " '$100 billion' more."
Hillary Rodham Clinton

September 1993, regarding assumed savings in Medicare and Medicaid under the Clinton plan: "It's fantasy . . . These numbers all come out of their computer in that way. They won't last, they mustn't last."
Democratic Senator and Chairman of Senate Finance Committee Daniel Patrick Moynihan

Health Care Choice

October 23, 1991: "People don't want some top-down bureaucracy telling them what to do anymore."

October 1993: [Some recommendations from the draft of Bill and Hillary Rodham Clinton's health care plan:

- "The National Health Board, the Department of Labor, and the Department of Health and Human Services are authorized to issue any regulation [pertaining to the health care law] . . . on an interim and final basis.

- Pharmaceutical manufacturers would be precluded from providing discounts to purchasers . . .

- The new provision calls for punishment for the receipt of any item of value as an inducement for referral of any type of health care business.

- States may establish one, and only one, regional [health care] alliance in each area."]

Health Care, Federal Role in

September 24, 1992: "We've got to quit having the Federal Government try to micromanage health care."

Some of Bill and Hillary Rodham Clinton's proposals for health care reform in 1992–1993:

- National board to establish regulations for every state, and to set ceiling for total health care costs

- National spending targets for health care expenditures

- Mandatory employer coverage of employees

- National council to certify the number of doctors permitted to train in medical specialities such as surgery

- 50 state fee schedules for medical services

- Controls over insurance premiums

- Price controls for over-the-counter drugs]

June 13, 1993: "I can understand how many of you [doctors] must feel when, instead of being trusted for your expertise, you're expected to . . . get approval for even basic medical procedures from a total stranger."
Hillary Rodham Clinton

Health Care Plan, Accurately Predicting Impact of

September 1993: "There shouldn't be any debate on the validity of these numbers."
Chairman of the White House National Economic Council Bob Rubin

September 1993: ". . . [we used] the most sophisticated [computer] models in the business of analyzing health care . . ."
Budget Director Leon Panetta

October 6, 1993: ". . . we just don't have the [computer forecast] modeling capabilities."
Chairwoman of the Council of Economic Advisers Laura Tyson

Health Care Plan, Percentage of People Paying More under

[In the Fall of 1993, members of the Clinton Administration gave varying estimates for the proportion of people who would have to pay more under the Clinton health care plan:]

September 1993: ". . . this was the first time that the financial experts on health care and all of the different Government agencies had ever been required to sit in a room together and agree on numbers."

September 21, 1993: "32 percent."
Top health care adviser Ira Magaziner

October 28, 1993: ". . . a few people will pay more."
Secretary of Health and Human Services Donna Shalala

Same testimony: "40 percent."
Secretary of Health and Human Services Donna Shalala

Same day: "One hundred percent of the people benefit from this plan."

November 1, 1993: "So let's stop this nonsense about who pays and who doesn't pay."
Hillary Rodham Clinton

November 4, 1993: "30 percent."
Budget Director Leon Panetta

Health Care Plan, Timetable for

November 20, 1991: "In the first year of the Clinton Administration, Congress and I will deliver quality, affordable health care for all Americans."

September 9, 1992: "[I will] offer, within the first one hundred days of taking office, a comprehensive health care plan . . ."

February 17, 1993: "Later this spring . . . I will deliver to Congress a comprehensive plan for health care reform . . ."

June 17, 1993: "I personally am getting quite close to making the final choices from among the options there."

July 29, 1993: "The exact timing is still under discussion."
White House health spokesman Robert O. Boorstin

Late Summer 1993: ". . . I think we have a chance to pass something this year."

October 12, 1993: "We don't have a hard deadline on it."
Press Secretary Dee Dee Myers

October 27, 1993: "I ask that before the Congress finishes its work next year . . . I sign a [health care] bill . . ."

October 28, 1993: "The debate is no longer over whether we will do something, but . . . how soon we can get it done."
  Hillary Rodham Clinton

Health Care Task Force, Closed Meetings of Hillary Rodham Clinton's

October 1991: "I would bring in all the players . . . and tell them to develop a national health care plan."

March 10, 1993, from Federal ruling that ordered task force to hold meetings which are open to the public: ". . . the court takes no pleasure in determining that one of the first actions taken by a president [holding closed meetings] is in direct violation of [the law]."

Same day: "[The president is] very gratified. The court has given its stamp of approval to everything the health care task force has done . . ."
  Communications Director George Stephanopoulos

March 22, 1993, in appealing the court's decision: "The Justice Department feels that the court made substantial errors both in interpreting and in applying the principles of constitutional law."
  Clinton Administration statement

September 22, 1993: ". . . I have been deeply moved by the spirit of this [health care] debate, by the openness of all people to new ideas and argument and information."

July 1992: "I'd like to think of ways to open up the White House."
  Hillary Rodham Clinton

Health Care Taxes

1992: "We don't need . . . a tax increase that asks hard-working people who already pay too much for health care to pay even more."
Clinton campaign issue brief

August 12, 1992: "There will be a buy-in, which they can call a payroll tax [for health care] . . ."

August 25, 1992: "We haven't proposed any payroll tax."
Al Gore

February 21, 1993: "I think there is a possibility that with regard to . . . alcohol and tobacco and so forth, that Americans may be asked to bear a small part of the health care costs."
Labor Secretary Robert Reich

March 23, 1993: "In terms of how it will be paid for, let me say that no decision has been made . . ."

April 14, 1993: ". . . [health care is] going to take some more resources, and a VAT [value-added tax] or a general sales tax has a good deal to recommend it."
Deputy Director of the Office of Management and Budget Alice Rivlin

July 31, 1993: "At least at the present time, I don't think we need to look at that [another tax] as a way of financing health care reform."

September 28, 1993, during Congressional session:

Question: ". . . do you think the Administration would consider taking . . . caffeine, cholesterol, salt, sugar, alcohol . . . and putting a tax on those..?"
Congressman Jim Bunning

Answer: "If there is a way that you can ever come up with to tax substances like the ones you've just named, we'll be glad to look at it."
Hillary Rodham Clinton

Hispanic for the Supreme Court, Nominating an

July 1, 1992: "The old adage, *mi casa, su casa,* will be true when my house is the White House . . . I certainly will give every consideration to Hispanic candidates for the Supreme Court."

June 1993: [The "short list," or strongly considered names of candidates, for the Supreme Court post made available in March 1993 were: Stephen Breyer, Bruce Babbitt, Richard Riley, Mario Cuomo, and Ruth Bader Ginsburg.]

Hussein, Saddam

October 19, 1992: ". . . we sent him [Saddam Hussein] some sort of communication on the eve of his invasion of Kuwait that we still wanted better relations. So I think that was wrong."

January 13, 1993: "I think a couple of times over the last year and a half we have sent mixed signals. I think that the hope is we will send a firm and consistent set of signals."

Next sentence: "So let me just say I wouldn't rule out reviewing our options [with Saddam Hussein] in the future . . . we'll see what happens over the next several days and we'll take it from there."

Same interview: "But the main thing is we can't do anything to give him or anyone else the slightest indication that we are wavering."

ॠ ॠ ॠ

I

Influence Peddling

November 20, 1991: "For too many Americans, for too long, it's seemed that Congress and the White House have been more interested in looking out for themselves and for their friends, but not for the country . . ."

February 6, 1993: "We're going to take on the lobbyists for the special interests that have grown used to getting special favors from our government."

May and June 1993: [The "Congressional Dinner" which Bill Clinton hosted with leaders of Congress charged $15,000 a table for 1,800 guests such as heads of unions and corporations. Clinton's "President's Dinner" charged lobbyist invitees an identical table fee of $15,000.]

ন&&   ন&&   ন&&

J

Jackson, Jesse, President's Temper and

December 1993: "I think the trick of being in public life in this day and age . . . is to be able to take all this barrage of criticism seriously but not personally."

January 26, 1992, upon being told, falsely, that Jesse Jackson was supporting another Presidential candidate: "It's an outrage, it's a dirty, double-crossing, back-stabbing thing to do . . . Everything he has bragged about, he has gushed to me about trust and trust and trust, and it's a back-stabbing thing to do."

February 27, 1992: "I didn't fly off the handle."

Next sentence: "I just used strong words to describe how I felt at that moment."

Japan Summit, Results from

July 8, 1993: "What distinguishes this summit is that we've moved beyond the promise to the payoff—a breakthrough in these [trade] negotiations that is much more than an agreement to agree."
Treasury Secretary Lloyd Bentsen

July 10, 1993: "We should have no illusions. We announce today a framework to govern specific agreements yet to be negotiated."

Job Discrimination by Race or Gender

September 1992: "[We oppose] racial quotas . . . [we would] ban gender-based discrimination in federal hiring . . ."

April 23, 1993: "I believe that this country's policies should be heavily biased in favor of nondiscrimination."

November 12, 1993: "White House personnel . . . is deeply entrenched against 'white male career officers.'"
State Department Undersecretary for Management Richard Moose

[Of the first 33 federal judges selected by Bill Clinton in 1993, 21 (64 percent) were women or minorities.]

Job Quotas for Women

October 23, 1991: "For 12 years, this President and his predecessor have divided us against each other—pitting . . . women against men."

February 29, 1992: "I would not restrict myself to having just half the Cabinet [be] women; I might want more."

August 1992: "There's no reason for us to be dividing women against women or men against women. This country needs people who want to reach beyond these boundaries and quit pointing fingers at one another."
Hillary Rodham Clinton

December 21, 1992, in chastising women's groups for demanding more female appointees: "[They're] bean counters . . . They're playing quota games and math games . . . There are more than numbers at stake here."

Same news conference, when asked to estimate the final number of women in his Cabinet: "[M]ore than three."

Jobs Bill, Cost of

January 27, 1993: "Whether it's $15 billion, $20 billion or $25 billion is still very unclear."
    Labor Secretary Robert Reich

Same day, on estimate of $31 billion: "[It's] in the ballpark."
    Communications Director George Stephanopoulos

Same day: "Among the figures discussed were $16 billion, $18 billion, $24 billion, $31 billion, $32 billion, zero, and a lot more. It is factually incorrect and highly misleading to suggest that any decision has been made or any one figure or any one approach has been determined."
    Senate Majority Leader George Mitchell

Jogging Track on White House Lawn

[In February 1993, while construction crews and equipment built, in full view of photographers, a jogging track on the White House grounds, the following exchange took place between reporters and Bill Clinton's press secretary Dee Dee Myers:]

Question: "Are you building a jogging track out here?"

Answer: "I'm looking into that and we'll have an answer for you on that later . . . I'm looking into it and we'll get back to you."

Q: "What does that mean, looking into it?.."

A: "We're looking into it and as soon as I can tell you with some specificity—no, but as soon as I can tell you with some specificity what the details are, I will let you know. I can't do that right now."

Q: "How about a simple yes or no answer?"

A: "I will get back to you."

Q: "Are they building a jogging track out there?"

A: "I will get back to you . . ."

Q: ". . . [I]t probably costs something and one wonders how much."

A: "As I'm sure you know, things are not always as they appear."

Junk Food, Bill Clinton and

1979: "[Children] might have special standing to question the proliferation of nuclear power or junk food because of the . . . unpredictable impact on their and their children's future development."
  Hillary Rodham Clinton

April 1993: "I don't necessarily consider McDonald's junk food . . . They have salads."

November 9, 1993: "People say to me, 'President Clinton, he jogs straight to McDonald's.' I say, 'Now, Mr. President, I'm not saying I'm totally against fast food, but you . . . you take it in moderation!"
  Co-chairwoman of the President's Council on Physical Fitness Florence Griffith Joyner

Jury Selection, Fairness in

[In February 1993, a federal judge denied an attempt by the Clinton Justice Department to select, on the basis of ethnicity, a new jury for the trial of Democratic Congressman Harold Ford of Tennessee.]

February 22, 1993: "It is a sad day, in my view, when the acting Attorney General and a representative of the White House give in

to a demand that a jury of the United States must be selected by race . . ."
  U.S. District Court Judge Jerome Turner

Next day: "Although the [Justice Department of the] United States joined in the defendant's motion . . . to select a new jury panel"

Next phrase: "we believe that the District Court acted well within its discretion."
  Clinton Justice Department statement

ᣟ   ᣟ   ᣟ

K

Kosher Kitchen in the White House

March 29, 1992, before Jewish audience: "[I would] keep a glatt [strict] kosher kitchen in the White House."

August 12, 1993: "We don't serve kosher meals on a regular basis."
   Worker in White House kitchen

L

Labor Unions

November 7, 1993, in complaining about union lobbying against the NAFTA trade agreement: ". . . the vociferous, organized opposition of most of the unions telling these [Congressional] members in private they'll never give them any money again . . . the real roughshod, muscle-bound tactics."

Moments later: "I mean, those guys [in the unions] are my friends."

Lieutenant Governor's Race in Arkansas

[In July 1993, a Republican candidate won the Arkansas Lieutenant Governor's race.]

July 28, 1993: "It was not a referendum on the President or his program . . . it was a local race on local issues."
   Press Secretary Dee Dee Myers

Same day: "There was a very hostile climate out there to the Democratic Party in general, and to Bill Clinton in particular."
   Defeated Democratic candidate Nate Coulter

Limbaugh, Rush, Armed Forces Broadcast of

Fall 1993: *"The Rush Limbaugh Show* [on radio] makes no pretense that his show is balanced. If AFRTS [Armed Forces Radio and Television Service] scheduled a program of personal commentary without balancing it with another viewpoint, we would be open to broad criticism that we are supporting a particular point of view."
Defense Department statement

December 2, 1993: "We'll broadcast his radio show as soon as we can legally do so."
AFRTS Deputy Director Melvin Russell

Line Item Veto for the Federal Budget

June 1992: ". . . I am strongly in favor of the line-item veto . . ."

November 16, 1992, 13 days after the election: ". . . [House Speaker Tom Foley] made an intriguing suggestion . . . I can line-item-veto a bill here [in Washington] and the legislature can override it with a majority vote."

Lobbying, "Revolving Door" between Government Service and

1992, during campaign: "I think we should make it much more difficult for people to walk out of a government job and start lobbying."

February 17, 1993: "The American people have a right to know who is lobbying their Government leaders . . ."

December 1993: [White House Deputy Chief of Staff Roy Neel resigned to become head of an organization that lobbies the federal government, the United States Telephone Association. The head of the White House Congressional Liaison Office, Howard Paster, resigned to join Hill and Knowlton, a public relations and lobbying firm.]

December 8, 1993: "I don't think we should discourage people from moving in and out of government . . ."

December 1993: "There is a standard [of ethics], the President expects everybody to abide by it, and beyond that, I don't have anything to say about it."
    Press Secretary Dee Dee Myers

January 25, 1994: "So I also must now call on [Congress to pass] . . . tough and meaningful . . . lobby reform legislation. . . ."
    1994 State-of-the-Union speech

Lobbyists

September 1992: "The last 12 years were nothing less than an extended hunting season for high-priced lobbyists and Washington influence peddlers. On streets where statesmen once strolled, a never-ending stream of money now changes hands—tying the hands of those elected to lead."

February 15, 1993: "Many have already lined the corridors of power with high-priced lobbyists."

[Some high-ranking Clinton officials who had been engaged in lobbying:
  • CIA Director R. James Woolsey
  • Commerce Secretary Ron Brown
  • Head of Congressional Liason Office Howard Paster
  • Energy Secretary Hazel O'Leary
  • Trade Representative Mickey Kantor]

Los Angeles Riots, Blame for

April 30, 1992, in the aftermath of the violence in South Central Los Angeles: "[Republicans supported] more than a decade of urban decay."

May 1, 1992: "I don't think today is the day for us to be casting stones and placing blame."

Los Angeles Riots, Responsibility for Looting during

May 1, 1992: "I would show no sympathy for the violation of the law . . ."

May 10, 1992: "Oh, to be sure, it was heartbreaking to see some little children going into the stores in Los Angeles and stealing from their neighbors. But they live in a country where the top 1 percent of Americans have more wealth than the bottom 90 percent."

ૐ ૐ ૐ

M

Marijuana, Smoking

July 1991: "[I've never] broken any drug law."

March 29, 1992: "I've never broken a state law."

Next sentence: "But when I was in England I experimented with marijuana a time or two,"

Same sentence: "and I didn't like it. I didn't inhale it, and never tried it again."

Same day, in response to query on past drug use: "Nobody's ever asked me that question point-blank."

Meaning, Communication, and the First Lady

Spring 1993: "We have to first create a language that would better communicate what we have to say . . . to come to grasp with some of the inarticulate, maybe even inarticulable, things that we're feeling."

Spring 1993: "I hope one day to be able to stop long enough actually to try to write down what I do mean, because it's important to me that I try to do that, because I have floated around the edges of this and talked about it for many, many years . . ."

July 1993: "One of the things I have learned in the last seven or eight months is that meaning is imputed into things I do and say that's beyond me."

Media, Attitude on the

Fall 1993: "Some of them [in the media] got in their mind that I didn't like the press, which is not true."

Same interview: "So the press decided for whatever reason that they would deny me a [political] honeymoon."

Three sentences later: "I just have no criticism of it [the media]."

Two questions later: "I have a bigger quarrel, by the way, with the media . . ."

Same interview: "Do I care if I get credit [from the media]? No."

Same response: "And you get no credit around here [from the media] for fighting and bleeding."

Medical Records, Releasing the President's

October 9, 1992: "We feel that this a privacy issue and that if he became President, his medical records would be open."
   Clinton spokeswoman Avis LaVelle

[On February 1, 1993, President Clinton fired his White House doctor, who claimed he was let go for refusing to give Clinton allergy shots without first seeing the President's medical records. The records remained closed to public scrutiny.]

Medicare

June 9, 1993, to business audience: ". . . there's about $60 billion in cuts from Medicare [in the proposed budget] . . ."

August 3, 1993: ". . . we must protect older Americans from punitive cuts in Social Security, Medicare, and veterans' benefits that some have proposed."

Middle-Class Tax Cut

January 9, 1992: "I'm Bill Clinton, and I believe you deserve more than 30-second ads or vague promises . . . [My economic plan] starts with a tax cut for the middle class."

June 17, 1992: "I'm going to have to at least modify but not abandon my position, and I'm still working on it."

June 19, 1992: "The press and my political opponents always made more of the middle-class tax cut than I ever did in my speeches."

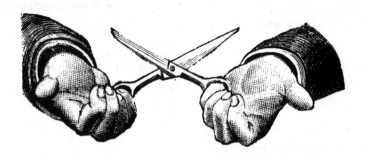

[In September of 1992, Bill Clinton made various proposals for a children's tax credit for middle-income workers, a "significant reduction" in middle-class income taxes, and a 10 percent cut in middle-class taxes.]

October 19, 1992: "I'm not going to raise taxes on middle-class Americans to pay for the programs I recommended . . . you know how you can trust me about that? . . . The person responsible . . . in my administration will be Bill Clinton."

January 14, 1993: "I never did meet any voter who thought that [that a middle-class tax cut was a priority]."

February 17, 1993: "To middle-class Americans who have paid a great deal for the last 12 years and from whom I ask a contribution tonight . . ."

May 17, 1993: "I've got four years—give me four years to deliver on the middle-class tax cut."

July 31, 1993: "I pledged . . . to seek the least possible burden on middle-income taxpayers . . ."

Mileage Standards for Cars

April 22, 1992, during 'Earth Day' speech: "We'll seek . . . to raise the average goal for automakers to 40 miles per gallon by the year 2000 . . ."

August 21, 1992, in backing away from the goal before industry group in Detroit: "I don't think it's fair to impose a burden on an American fleet that has bigger cars in it than foreign competitors do."

Millionaires Tax
(A Million Ain't Worth What It Used to Be)

September 1992: "[Impose] surtax on millionaires."

February 17, 1993: "We recommend a 10 percent surtax on incomes over $250,000 . . ."

[In August 1993, Congress approved Bill Clinton's proposal for a 10 percent surtax on earnings of $250,000 or more.]

"Murphy Brown Show,"
Dan Quayle's Remarks about

May 19, 1992: "[The Murphy Brown character is] mocking the importance of fathers by bearing a child alone, and calling it just another 'lifestyle choice.'"
Vice-President Dan Quayle

Same day: "The world is a much more complicated place than Dan Quayle wants to believe. He should watch a few episodes [of "Murphy Brown"] before he decides to pop off."
Clinton Campaign spokeswoman Dee Dee Myers

May 20, 1992: ". . . there's a lot of violence on television that may have a bigger impact on what happened in Los Angeles [the LA riot] than Murphy Brown's sitcom."

Same response: "I agree that [out-of-wedlock births are] not the example we want to set for our children."

Next day: ". . . it [Quayle's statement] ignores the relationship of our family problems to our national economic decline."

Same address: "Like any parent, I'm troubled by the gratuitous violence and sex and mixed moral signals on television."

April 6, 1993: ". . . the debate over family values over the last year, which was devised for political purposes, seemed so off-point."
Hillary Rodham Clinton

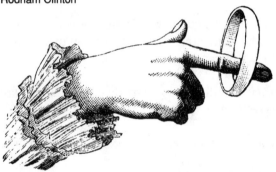

December 3, 1993: "I read his [Dan Quayle's] whole speech, the 'Murphy Brown' speech. I thought there were a lot of good things in that speech. I think he got too cute with 'Murphy Brown,' but it is certainly true that this country would be better off if our babies were born into two-parent families."

❧　　❧　　❧

N

NAFTA (North American Free Trade Agreement)

December 12, 1991: "And I supported giving the [Bush]Administration fast-track authority [free of outside interference] to negotiate a sound and fair free trade agreement with Mexico."

August 21, 1992: "I'm reviewing it [the trade treaty] carefully, and when I have a definite opinion I will say so."

October 19, 1992: "You know, Mr. Bush was very grateful when I was among the Democrats who said he ought to have the authority to negotiate an agreement with Mexico."

Next sentence: "Neither I nor anybody else, as far as I know, agreed to give him our proxy . . ."

Next sentence: "I am the one who's in the middle on this."

September 14, 1993, with George Bush and other former Presidents at his side, Bill Clinton finally proclaimed open support for the treaty: "These men . . . join us today because we all recognize the important stakes for our nation in this issue."

October 4, 1993, before labor audience opposed to the treaty: "[The treaty is a] symbol of the legitimate grievances of the American working people about the way they've been worked over."

November 1, 1993, in support of NAFTA: "I would jump on this [treaty] like flies on a June bug."

NAFTA, Deals Made to Win Passage of

November 1993: "The people that I've talked to in Congress have been nobly motivated."

October-November 1993: [Some of the items Bill Clinton agreed to to win votes for NAFTA "free trade" agreement:

- Joint U.S.-Mexican bank with $2.9 billion in funding, for one Congressman
- Two C-17 cargo planes, costing $1.4 billion, for one Congresswoman
- Over 2,000 pages of trade regulations
- Greater protection for the asparagus, beef, brandy, broom maker, celery, citrus, cucumber, flat glass, home appliance, lettuce, manhole maker, peanut, peanut butter, pipe fitting, sugar, television, tomato, wheat, and wine industries
- 136 customs agents for the textile industry
- $33 million for an agricultural research station in Florida, and $10 million to accelerate construction of a "Center for the Study of Western Hemispheric Trade" in Texas]

"Nannygate" (Non-Payment of Social Security Taxes for Household Help)

October 15, 1992: ". . . you have to . . . [ask] the wealthiest Americans . . . to pay their fair share of taxes."

[It was reported during 1993 that many Clinton officials and nominees did not pay required Social Security taxes on their nannies or babysitters. These people included:

- Shirley Chater, nominee to head the Social Security Administration
- Lawrence Thompson, nominee for deputy head of Social Security Administration

- Zoe Baird, first Attorney General nominee
- Kimba Wood, second Attorney General nominee
- Ron Brown, Secretary of Commerce
- Federico Pena, Secretary of Transportation
- Bobby Ray Inman, second Defense Secretary nominee]

[The following Clinton Administration personnel may not have paid Social Security taxes for a nurse hired during 1981–82 to care for their daughter:

- Bill Clinton
- Hillary Rodham Clinton

This cannot be confirmed or refuted, as the Clintons have declined to release their tax records from this period.]

"Nannygate" and Standards in Federal Hiring

September 1992: "[I support] efforts . . . to ban gender-based discrimination in federal hiring . . ."

1993: [Of all Clinton nominees who violated laws for payment of taxes on domestic help, the nominations of only two were withdrawn for that reason. The two—Zoe Baird and Kimba Wood—were both women.]

National Police Force

September 7, 1993: "Transfer law enforcement functions of the Drug Enforcement Administration [DEA] . . . to the Federal Bureau of Investigation."
    Al Gore, report on "reinventing government"

September 8, 1993, in downplaying the recommendation: ". . . just to reorganize something because it sounds good doesn't necessarily produce the results that you seek."
Attorney General Janet Reno

September 29, 1993: "Clearly, the vision of successfully combining the best of the FBI and the DEA into a single drug-enforcement unit is truly awesome."
Deputy Attorney General Philip Heymann

October 21, 1993, on the Gore report's recommendation: ". . . a printing error."
Deputy Attorney General Philip Heymann

National Service, Financing College through

October 6, 1992: "We offer a solution—a national trust fund out of which any American can borrow the money to finance a college education, no questions asked."

February 3, 1993: "President Clinton is planning to unveil a small pilot program allowing some college students to repay government loans through community service."
Eli Segal, head of national service initiative

[On September 8, 1993, the Senate approved a bill, supported by Bill Clinton, to provide funding for about 30,000 students annually (approximately 1.4 million high school graduates enroll in college each year).]

"New Covenant"

[The "New Covenant" was Bill Clinton's campaign catch-all phrase to describe his philosophy of government.]

November 20, 1991: "This New Covenant isn't liberal or conservative."

Next sentence: "It's both"

Next phrase: "and it's different."

Nominees to High Office, Speed in Confirming

May 27, 1993: "... I was the first President since anybody could remember that had every other member of his Cabinet confirmed the day after I took office."

[In 1969, Richard Nixon's entire Cabinet was confirmed on Inauguration Day. In 1961, John Kennedy's entire Cabinet was confirmed on the day after Inauguration Day.]

North Korea, the Nuclear Bomb and

November 3, 1993: "The ball is now in North Korea's court."
Defense Secretary Les Aspin

November 7, 1993: "North Korea cannot be allowed to develop a nuclear bomb. We have to be very firm about it ... This is a very grave issue for the United States."

December 7, 1993: "Clearly, the ball is in our court at this point."
Press Secretary Dee Dee Myers

December 12, 1993: "... [the North Koreans] might at this moment possess a single nuclear device ... We are comfortable now ... they are not building the potential for more bombs."
Defense Secretary Les Aspin

December 17, 1993: "We in no sense are tolerating a nuclear program in North Korea."
    Secretary of State Warren Christopher

December 1993: "We're just going to be firm"

Next phrase: "and keep the hand out at the same time"

Next phrase: "and hope it works."

Nuclear Bomb Materials, Banning Production of

September 27, 1993: "Growing global stockpiles of plutonium . . . are raising the danger of nuclear terrorism for all nations. We will press for an international agreement that would ban production of these materials for weapons forever."

October 20, 1993: "I have not, however, called for a treaty banning all fissile material production [of plutonium]. Such a proposal would breach existing U.S. commitments . . ."

O

Ozone Depletion

[The United States signed a treaty in 1990 to ban production of ozone-depleting chemicals by 1996.]

1992: ". . . yet even now, when the evidence against [ozone-depleting chemicals] is overwhelming, these life-threatening compounds are still being released into the atmosphere, and some countries still refuse to join the global effort to ban them."
    Al Gore

[In December of 1993, Bill Clinton asked the DuPont Co. to continue manufacture of an ozone-depleting substance for automobile air conditioners.]

"Given the relatively small change in the ozone layer [involved] . . . the equation for us was that it just didn't pay [to end production]."
    Paul Stolpman, Director of the Office of Atmospheric Programs for the Environmental Protection Agency

P

Pay Raise as Arkansas Governor

January 1992: "In 11 years as governor, I've never had a pay raise."

[During Governor Clinton's terms of office, 1979–80 and 1983–1992, the Arkansas constitution fixed the salary of the governor.]

Pay Raise for Congress

[In July 1991, the U.S. Senate's $23,200-per-member pay raise, enacted at night, provoked a storm of criticism among both the public and candidates for high office.]

January 16, 1992: "For 12 years the politicians in Washington have raised their pay . . . That's wrong."
Clinton campaign commercial

January 17, 1992: " '[Clinton] personally told me the pay raise was a good idea.'"
Democratic Congressmen David Obey

Perks and Privileges

[Between 1988 and 1990, Bill and Hillary Rodham Clinton received nine free airplane rides from the owner of Tyson Foods Inc., a multi-billion-dollar, Arkansas-based poultry business which received over $7 million in tax breaks from the Clinton state house, and upon whose board of directors Hillary Rodham Clinton sat.]

September 1992: "The privilege of public service ought to be enough of a perk for people in government."

Persian Gulf War, Congressional Vote on

January 1991, just before the start of the war with Iraq: "I agree with the arguments of the people in the minority on the resolution—that we should give sanctions more time and maybe even explore a full-scale embargo [and not authorize force against Iraq] . . ."

Same month: "I personally don't think it would have been a good thing for Congress to go on record, in essence, watering down and weakening the full impact of the U.N. resolution [to authorize force]."

Additional explanation: "I guess I would have voted with the majority if it was a close vote."

Next sentence: "But I agree with the arguments the minority made."

Different assertion: "[I was] an early and unambiguous supporter of [President Bush's] use of force against the Iraqi army."

Personnel Files, Rifling of

[In November 1992, Bill Clinton commented on the search of his passport files by the Bush Administration's State Department:]

"I just want you to know that the State Department of this country is not going to be fooling with Bill Clinton's politics, and if I catch them doing it [as President], I will fire them the next day."

[On September 9, 1993, the following response was made to a Congressional letter of inquiry about the reported search of files belonging to 160 former State Department officials of the Bush Administration:]

"We haven't responded to that letter yet . . . It has been assigned. I don't detect any sense of urgency in responding to it."
    Justice Department spokesman John Russell

[On November 10, 1993, two months after the start of a Justice Department investigation, two Clinton officials were dismissed over the personnel files. Unlike the Clinton passport case in the Bush Administration, the president did not appoint a special prosecutor to look further into the affair.]

Police, Adding 100,000

October 1992: ". . . provide 100,000 more police officers . . ."

[Bill Clinton proposed in August of 1993 a crime package with funds to pay for only 13,000 police. Many of the funded positions he referred to as "officers" are in fact "non-sworn"personnel such as security guards.]

October 24, 1993: "I said up to 50,000 [police]."
    Attorney General Janet Reno

Political Insider

Fall 1991: "I don't know how I could be an insider. I've never had a Washington job."

[On February 26, 1993, Bill Clinton recalled this 1965 incident from his undergraduate college days:] "Senator Fulbright's administrative assistant called me one morning in Arkansas and asked me if I wanted a job working for the Senate Foreign Relations Committee [in Washington, DC] as an assistant clerk . . . The next week . . . I was there working . . ."

"Pork Barrel" Programs

March 23, 1993, on whether his economic package contained wasteful projects: "No. Let me say, you will read those bills for years in vain and not find those projects."

February-August 1993: [Some of the items approved or proposed under Bill Clinton's budgets:

- $2.6 billion in payments to farmers not to grow crops
- $33 million for the Essential Air Service, which subsidizes airlines for flights to vacation resorts
- Helium reserve for a non-existent blimp industry
- Funds for projects in the affluent communities of Beverly Hills, California and East Hampton, New York
- $1.4 million for drawings of "significant structures and engineering achievements"]

Poverty, Fighting

September 1992: ". . . support new anti-poverty initiatives that move beyond the outdated answers of both major parties and instead reflect the values most Americans share: work, family, individual responsibility, community."

[Bill Clinton's proposals on poverty (in April 1993) included this expansion of traditional welfare programs: an increase in welfare, food stamps, and jobless benefits which was $4 billion more than Congress' budget request, and $15 billion more than the Bush Administration's 1993 request.]

R

Reinventing Government

[In 1990 and 1991, Senator Al Gore compiled the highest and seventh-highest record of spending in the U.S. Senate, according to the National Taxpayers Union.]

March 3, 1993: [In appointing Al Gore to head a commission to recommend ways to reduce wasteful spending and to reorganize the federal government:] "I thank the Vice President for his willingness to lead this effort."

[Al Gore released a report on September 7, 1993 on "reinventing government" which outlines proposals for $108 billion in cost savings over five years.]

[On October 14, 1993, Budget Director Leon Panetta stated that previously announced steps account for $42 billion of the report's purported savings, and that $22 billion in other supposed savings may only amount to $5 billion.]

[On November 16, 1993, the Congressional Budget Office said Al Gore's specific claim of $5.9 billion in savings over the next five years would result in only $305 million in savings, with over half of that in tax and fee increases.]

September 7, 1993: "Public confidence in the federal government has never been lower."
Al Gore

Reinventing Government, Report on

[In his report on "reinventing government," Al Gore criticized excessive and expensive bureaucracy at the Transportation Department and government print shop for squandering $20,000 on drivers safety documents.]

September 7, 1993: "Here's a sad story about the Government Printing Office . . . and . . . wasted taxpayer money . . ."
Al Gore's report on "reinventing government"

[Because Al Gore's report of September 7, 1993 was printed on slick, multi-color paper, it cost over three times the amount of a normal government report. The expense of printing 64,500 copies of the Gore report was $168,915. In contrast, the cost of printing the same number of a regular government report would have been $54,091.]

Russia's Election, Reaction to Strong Showing by Radicals in

[On December 12, 1993, ultra-nationalists and Communists won the largest share of delegates in elections for Russia's new parliament. The party of Vladimir Zhirinovsky—who has spoken admiringly of Adolph Hitler, demanded the United States return Alaska to Russia and threatened to flood the Baltic states with radiation—received the most votes.]

December 13, 1993: "By approving a new constitution and voting for a new legislature, the Russian people have eliminated the last vestiges of the old Soviet system and replaced them with new and legitimate institutions that will lay a foundation for continued development of a democratic society."

January 6, 1994: "We would be foolish to ignore those [election] results. . . . There is . . . a dark cloud on Europe's horizon. It is the threat of fiery nationalism ignited by old resentments, fueled by economic frustration, fanned by self-serving demagogues."
Al Gore

ès   ès   ès

S

Savings and Loan, Madison, Role of Hillary Rodham Clinton in

[In March of 1992, the Clinton campaign denied that Hillary Rodham Clinton—in her capacity as senior partner for Little Rock's Rose law firm—provided Madison counsel on its dealings with the Arkansas Securities Department, a state regulatory agency.]

Same month: "[Hillary Rodham Clinton performed] some limited work . . . [and played a] limited role before the Securities Department . . ."
    Webster Hubbell, managing partner of Rose law firm, and later Bill Clinton's Associate Attorney General

School Choice

[Under "school choice," the government would provide parents with cash grants or vouchers to pay for their children's education, at a public or private school of their choice.]

October 18, 1990, in letter to advocate of school choice: "I am fascinated by that proposal [public school funds to pay for tuition at private schools] . . . I'm concerned that the traditional Democratic Party establishment has not given you more encouragement. The visionary is rarely embraced by the status quo."

July 7, 1992, during meeting with the National Education Association, an opponent of school choice: ". . . we shouldn't give our money away to private schools . . ."

School Chosen for Chelsea Clinton

April 1990: "[Chelsea] has always been in the public schools and always will be."
Hillary Rodham Clinton

October 15, 1992: "There are great public schools where there's public school choice . . ."

January 5, 1993: [Bill Clinton announced he would place his daughter Chelsea Clinton in Washington, D.C.'s elite Sidwell Friends private school, where the yearly tuition is $10,400:]

"[This is] not a rejection of the District of Columbia's public schools,"
Communications Director George Stephanopoulos

Next phrase: "but the result of an effort to make sure the family found the right environment for their daughter."

Further explanation: ". . . Governor Clinton supports the public school system, as he has throughout his term of Governor and will continue as President."
Communications Director George Stephanopoulos

Scratch on President's Chin

April 5, 1993: "The President cut himself shaving."
Press Secretary Dee Dee Myers

Same day: "[H]e was playing with Chelsea, and I guess he just got scratched."
Communications Director George Stephanopoulos

Secretary of State, Resting Habits of the

[At the NATO summit in January 1994, Secretary of State Warren Christopher—in full view of photographers—slept during a speech by Bill Clinton. Members of Christopher's entourage had varying explanations for his doze:]

January 9, 1994: "Work. He was up all night. He should get a life."
Aide to Secretary of State Warren Christopher

Same day: "He was deep in thought."
Another aide to Secretary of State Warren Christopher

Segregated Country Club, Playing Golf at

March 20, 1992: "A guy asked me to play nine holes of golf. It was the only place we had time to play."

Next sentence: "I should not have done it."

Serving Out Term as Governor

April 10, 1990: "I don't know how many times I have to say it—I will serve four years as governor. As far as I'm concerned it's a bogus issue."

October 3, 1991: "Today I am declaring my candidacy for President of the United States."

Sesame Street (Watching One's Peas and Cues)

[During a taping of "Sesame Street" in October 1993, Hillary Rodham Clinton substituted the word *apple* for *peas* in the television script:]

October 14, 1993: "Hardly anyone likes peas."
    Hillary Rodham Clinton

October 15, 1993: "Mrs. Clinton is a pea lover and she agrees with Big Bird and was only trying to make sure fruits were included for nutritional value."
    Neel Lattimore, spokesman for Hillary Rodham Clinton

Sexual Restraint

1992: "We taught them what to do in the front seat [of a car]. Now it's time to teach them what to do in the back seat."
    Joycelyn Elders, later Bill Clinton's Surgeon General

July 23, 1993: "The only thing that works 100 percent is abstinence."
    Surgeon General nominee Joycelyn Elders

October 19, 1993: "[America is] a repressed, Victorian society that misrepresents information, denies sexuality early . . ."
    National AIDS Policy Coordinator Kristine Gebbie

October 21, 1993: "Abstinence is the surest prevention of HIV transmission."
National AIDS Policy Coordinator Kristine Gebbie

November 9, 1993: ". . . sex is a good and pleasurable way of life."
National AIDS Policy Coordinator Kristine Gebbie

Small Business

November 20, 1991: "Most new jobs in this country are created by small businesses and entrepreneurs who get little help from the government."

1993, regarding effect of health care plan on smaller firms: "I cannot be responsible for saving every undercapitalized entrepreneur in America."
Hillary Rodham Clinton

Social Security

[On February 25, 1986, Bill Clinton endorsed a resolution by the National Governors Association which entailed cuts in cost-of-living increases for Social Security.]

September 1, 1992: "We're not going to fool with Social Security. It's solid. It's secure. It's sound. And I'm going to keep it that way . . . You can take that one to the bank."

January 28, 1993: "[A cut in Social Security cost-of-living increases] is one of the issues that's being discussed. We haven't made any final decision yet."
Communications Director George Stephanopoulos

February 17, 1993: "[T]he [budget] plan does ask older Americans with higher incomes who do not rely solely on Social

Security to get by to contribute more [in higher Social Security taxes]."

Somali Warlord Mohamed Aidid

June 17, 1993, in commenting about a U. N. raid on Aidid's headquarters: "The purpose of the operation was to undermine the ability of Aidid to wreak military havoc in Somalia. The military back of Aidid has been broken. A warrant has been issued for his arrest."

October 5, 1993, two days after Aidid's men kill 18 U.S.soldiers: "We never went there to win a fight with Aidid . . ."

October 8, 1993: "We're not going to tolerate people messing with us."

Next sentence: "But we need to state unambiguously that our job is not to decide who gets to play a role in . . . Somalia."

Same day: "And, of course, I wouldn't rule out an operation against Aidid if the opportunity presented itself."
Secretary of Defense Les Aspin

October 10, 1993: "[. . . the U.S. envoy to Somalia] should be stimulating the political process."
U.S. Ambassador to the United Nations Madeleine Albright

October 14, 1993: ". . . there must be some resolution of the unconscionable incident which started this whole thing, which was the murder [by Aidid's fighters] of 24 Pakistani peacekeepers . . ."

December 2, 1993: [A U.S. airplane and armored personnel carrier escorted Aidid to talks between warring Somali factions.]

December 6, 1993: "Everyone thought it was important that General Aidid go to that peace conference."

Somalia, U.S. Troops in

October 11, 1992: "I agree we cannot commit ground forces to become involved . . . in the tribal wars of Somalia."

August 10, 1993: "[Our] goal [is] to have all American forces out of Somalia during 1994."
  David Shinn, State Department coordinator of Somalian policy

Same statement: "[U]nless there are a lot of setbacks."

September 17, 1993: "We have the troops there, and it certainly doesn't mean more troops there."

Same interview: "Our position is not well enough formed yet . . ."

September 28, 1993: "The country can basically be given back to the people who live there."

October 7, 1993: "And all around the world, aggressors, thugs, and terrorists will conclude that the best way to get us to change our policies is to kill our people. It would be open season on Americans."

South Africa, Ownership of Diamond Stocks in

1980-81: [Bill and Hillary Clinton filed joint tax returns which listed specific transactions on South African diamond stocks.]

July 8, 1992: ". . . all she [Hillary Clinton] can remember is she gave a discretionary account to a broker."

Next sentence: "She remembers little else except at some point she told the broker she didn't want that type of stock."
  Adviser to Clinton campaign Betsy Wright

July 13, 1992: "I wasn't aware of it [owning shares of DeBeer's mining stock]"

Same sentence: "but if it was true, we shouldn't have owned it,"

Next phrase: "and we only owned it for a while and we sold it,"

Next phrase: "but I didn't know that we did until I read about it in the papers."

Special Interests

September 1992: "We will eliminate taxpayer subsidies for narrow special interests."

[The following is a partial list of continuing special interest programs in the 1993 Clinton budget proposals:
- Appalachian Regional Commission
- Arts and public broadcasting
- Highway demonstration projects
- Loan credits for exporting firms
- Farm income supports]

Spelling, Skill in

April 19, 1993: ". . . *establishe* a bipartisan National *Eduation* Goals Panel to report on progress toward *achieveing* the goals."
Memo from Bill Clinton on reform of education

September 8, 1993: "Don't have to be a good speller to get the job."
Joke by Al Gore, on *Late Show With David Letterman,* a gibe which mocked Dan Quayle's spelling ability

September 13, 1993, from official program at Israeli-Palestinian peace ceremony: "Yitzhak Rabin Prime Minister of *Isreal*"

Spending Cuts

February 17, 1993: "[The budget seeks] cuts, not gimmicks, in government spending."

Same day: [In his first budget proposal, Bill Clinton's "spending cuts" included the following:

- Higher taxes on items such as Social Security benefits
- Fee increases, like charges for veterans' loans
- Income from federal auctions of radio frequency licenses
- Reductions in the rate of some increased spending
- Exclusion from the budget of billions of dollars to clean up bankrupt savings and loans
- Dragging out construction of federal science projects, with resulting higher total costs
- Increases in private sector financing of federal projects
- Increases in tax credits]

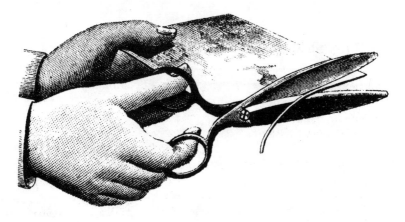

August 3, 1993: "You must wonder if these cuts are for real."

August 9, 1993: "And I plead guilty. There's a lot more spending cuts than spending, but there is some new spending."

October 14, 1993: "There is a tremendous trust deficit. We must prove to the American people that their hard-earned tax dollars will be treated with respect."
Budget Director Leon Panetta

Spending Cuts, Pledge for Major Round of

August 5, 1993: [In exchange for supporting his budget bill, Bill Clinton promised to support the effort of Congressional Democrats wanting to submit a substantial package of spending cuts later in the year.]

November 10, 1993: "Additional cuts would drain needed resources from other priority uses . . ."
Deputy Director of the Office of Management and Budget Alice Rivlin

T

Tax Hike in Arkansas, Stance on

[In his Fall 1986 campaign, Governor Bill Clinton vowed to oppose a general tax increase for Arkansas if he won reelection.]

January 6, 1987, after winning reelection: "I don't think anyone knew what the depth of the revenue crisis would be."

[On January 19, 1987, Governor Bill Clinton issued a report asking for $387 million in state "revenue increases."]

Taxes, Bill Clinton's Euphemisms for

"Contribution"

"User Fee"

"Responsibility"

"Spending Cut"

"Offsetting Collection"

"Higher Health Insurance Premiums"

"Reimbursable Obligation"

"Restoring Fairness"

"Employer Mandates"

"Undistributed Offsetting Receipt"

"Patriotism"

Taxes, General Attitude on

1991: "I think the country is moving toward a new maturity on taxes. Although there is still an enormous anti-tax feeling out there, people have come to the conclusion that we have to invest more in the nation."

August 21, 1992: "I reject [the] brain-dead politics of both parties . . . and the old Democratic orthodoxy that . . . we can tax and spend and regulate our way to prosperity."

February 15, 1993: ". . . more Americans must contribute [taxes] today so that all Americans can do better tomorrow."

Taxes, Paying Their Fair Share of

[The 1992 tax return of Bill and Hillary Rodham Clinton included the following deductions:

- Accelerated payment of Hillary Rodham Clinton's law firm profits, which enabled payment under a 1992 tax rate of 31 percent, instead of the 36-41 percent rates of Bill Clinton's economic proposals
- Exemption from federal taxes of $82,000 of investments in municipal bonds
- Exemption from federal and state taxes of $35,000 worth of Arkansas municipal bonds]

[The deductions on the Clintons' 1986 tax return included the following:

- 6 pair of socks: valued at $9
- 3 pair of used underwear: valued at $6]

Taxes, Threshold for Increased

October 11, 1992: "The tax increase I have proposed triggers in at family incomes of $200,000 and above."

January 19, 1993: "I now believe what I said might be true in the campaign, but I didn't think it was—that we have to raise it [the tax base] from a broader base than just people that make over $100,000 . . ."

February-August 1993: [Bill Clinton and Congress approved a gasoline tax that affects persons of *all* incomes, including the poorest, as would have his proposed BTU energy tax which was rejected. An increase in Social Security taxes affects couples earning more than $44,000 a year. A hike in income taxes triggers in for couples earning $140,000 in taxable income.]

Term Limits on Elected Officials

September 1990, in opposing term limits: "The people have enough sense to make these judgments at each election."

January 5, 1992: ". . . I wouldn't rule out term limits."

Same interview: "[I am] personally opposed to term limits for Congress. . . ."

Same interview: ". . . I'm not saying that five, six years from now, I would oppose it."

October 15, 1992: "I know they're popular but I'm against them."

Thomas, Clarence, Supreme Court Nomination of

[On October 12, 1991, Bill Clinton commented about the Senate hearings on Clarence Thomas and Anita Hill:]

"I don't see how he [Thomas] can be disqualified on it [Hill's allegations of sexual harassment] unless they're sure beyond a reasonable doubt that he did what was said."

Same remarks: "I have questions about his legal views, his constitutional views. I have mixed feelings about it."

Next sentence: "On the other hand, I don't know what the alternative is."

Same remarks: "[The hearings] called into question whether he [Thomas] had convictions that would be consistent. I just don't know what to say about that."

October 14, 1991: "He [Thomas] didn't have, in my opinion, the requisite breadth of experience and understanding . . ."

Same remarks, on how he would have voted on the nomination: "I'm not a Senator [with a vote]. I am a governor."

Toxic Waste

April 22, 1992: "Too often, on the environment, as on so many other issues, the Bush Administration has been reactive, rudderless, and expedient."

December 7, 1992, in speaking about huge waste incinerator in East Liverpool, Ohio: "Until all questions concerning compliance with state and federal law have been answered, it doesn't make sense to grant any permit [to incinerate possibly toxic waste]."
 Al Gore

March 10, 1993, in justifying permission to commence burning at the East Liverpool incinerator: "[The government's earlier decisions] incurred certain legal obligations . . . toward the [incinerator] company that had invested tens of millions of dollars."

Al Gore

Travel Office, Dismissal of Workers at White House

May 19, 1993: [Seven employees of the White House travel office were fired on charges of financial mismanagement. It was widely alleged that the dismissals were aimed at opening up slots for political associates of the President, and that the FBI and IRS had improperly taken part in the White House investigation of the office.]

May 21, 1993, in explaining the firings: "[We were] striving against inefficiency and mismanagement."

May 25, 1993: "[I] had nothing to do with any decision except to save the taxpayers . . ."

Same day: "[U]ltimately anything that happens in the White House is the responsibility of the President."

July 2, 1993: [The White House said it would reinstate five of the dismissed employees in other federal jobs, and that it had given reprimands to four Administration officials involved in the dismissals.]

Same day: [The official White House report on the travel office affair contained this apology:] "While all White House office employees serve at the pleasure of the President, . . ."

Next phrase: "the abrupt manner of dismissal of the Travel Office employees was unnecessary and insensitive."

Next sentence: "Although the . . . financial review provided ample justification to remove those with control over the Office's finances,"

Next phrase and sentence: "the removal need not have been so abrupt. All of the employees should have had an opportunity to hear the reasons for their termination . . ."

U

U.N. Control of U.S. Troops

[A draft presidential directive of July 14, 1993 called for placing various U.S. forces "under the operational control of a United Nations commander."]

October 14, 1993: "[Somalia] would make me more cautious about having any Americans in a peace-keeping role where there was any ambiguity at all about . . . decisions . . . made by a command other than an American command with direct accountability to the United States . . ."

December 1993: "The [U.N.] force commander will normally exercise operational control over all assigned units, including U.S. units. The commander has full command authority over operational and logistics matters . . ."
    Draft of U.S. Army manual

ea   ea   ea

V

Value-Added Tax (VAT)

[A value-added tax (VAT) is a tax placed on a product at each stage of its manufacture or assembly.]

February 19, 1993: "I do believe that America, at another time, and maybe not too long in the future, will debate whether we want to shift the nature of our tax system [to a VAT or sales tax]."

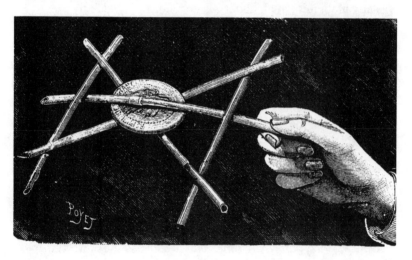

Same day: "It is not something that is now under consideration. If we start considering it, I'll tell you."

Same day: "I'm ruling it out for now. There's no discussion of it at this point."
Press Secretary Dee Dee Myers

February 1993: "There seems to be growing support for it."
Treasury Secretary Lloyd Bentsen

March 24, 1993: "I think the President ruled that out fairly clearly a couple of weeks ago."
Press Secretary Dee Dee Myers

April 13, 1993: "Certainly we're looking at a VAT."
Donna Shalala, Secretary of Health and Human Services

Next day: "If a decision is made to go forward with something like that, it's certainly something the president will explain and justify, but no decision has been made along those lines . . ."
Communications Director George Stephanopoulos

Same day: "I think a VAT has a good deal to recommend it."
Deputy Director of the Office of Management and Budget Alice Rivlin

April 16, 1993: "I personally don't think it's likely to occur in the near term. I've never been for that particular approach in concept."
Al Gore

July 31, 1993: ". . . we ought to have a debate on it [a VAT tax]; you know, there's a lot of support already in the Congress."

February 19, 1993: "[T]here's only so much change a country can accommodate at the same time."

Veterans' Benefits

August 25, 1992, before the American Legion: ". . . [I reject] the IRS' shameful attempt to tax cost-of-living adjustments to veterans disability payments."

1993: [Bill Clinton's proposed cuts in veterans' benefits included:

- Delay in cost-of-living allowances for military retirees
- Elimination of 1994 cost-of-living increase in grants under the GI Bill]

❧   ❧   ❧

W

Waco, Texas, Rationale for Final Federal Assault on Branch Davidian Compound in

April 23, 1993: "We know that David Koresh had sex with children. I think that is undisputed, is it not?"

Same day: ". . . Examinations of the children [in the compound] produced no indication of current or previous injuries.
Statement of Texas Child Protective Services office

Waco, Texas, Responsibility for Final Federal Assault on Branch Davidian Compound in

April 19, 1993: "I knew it [the assault] was going to be done, but the decisions were entirely hers [Attorney General Janet Reno's]."

Same day: "Of course the President takes responsibility for what's done in his government, but it is under the operational control of the Justice Department."
Communications Director George Stephanopoulos

Same day: "I made the decisions. I'm accountable. The buck stops with me."
Attorney General Janet Reno

Same day: "But the President is the President and he takes responsibility for it."
Press Secretary Dee Dee Myers

Same day: "It's not possible for a president to distance himself from things that happen when the federal government is in control."

Welfare Benefits, Time Limit on Receipt of

October 23, 1991: "We'll give them all the help they need for up to two years. But after that, if they're able to work, they'll have to take a job . . ."

February 1992: "I would go beyond two years [of providing benefits] if they [welfare recipients] were in a meaningful training program."

February 17, 1993: ". . . give people on welfare the education and training they need for up to two years, but after that, require all those who can work to go to work."

June 1993: "I'm not a believer in artificial deadlines of that nature."
Secretary of Housing and Urban Development Henry Cisneros

November 1, 1993: [Bill Clinton allowed the state of Wisconsin to try a pilot program limiting welfare payments to two years.]

June 1993: "I fear that time limits mean very different things to people in the Administration and to their audience, the public at large."
Democratic Senator Daniel Patrick Moynihan

Welfare Reform in Arkansas, Record of

Fall 1992: "In my state, we've moved 17,000 people from welfare rolls to payrolls."

[During the same period (1979–92) that 17,000 people in Arkansas left welfare, 51,000 people—three times as many—entered the state's welfare rolls.]

July 16, 1992: "And so I say to all those . . . who would criticize Arkansas: Come on down, especially if you're from Washington—come on down . . . you might even learn a thing or two."

Welfare Reform Program in Arkansas

[Bill Clinton said the following about Project Success, a Clinton welfare reform project in Arkansas:] "[It was rated] one of the three best programs in the country."

[The rating Clinton mentioned was actually given to a welfare reform program called WORK, established by former Arkansas governor Frank White.]

White House Staff, Cutting the

November 16, 1992: "I'm going to get out there [the White House] and set an example. I'm going to cut 25 percent from the White House staff."

January 12, 1993: "I don't know exactly how long that's going to take, but it's something we're pointing towards."
Communications Director George Stephanopoulos

February 15, 1993: ". . . I cut the White House staff by 25 percent . . ."

[For the 1994 budget year, Bill Clinton proposed a supplemental increase of $11.7 million, a 7.6 percent increase in White House funding, and 50 more employees. 117 White House employees characterized as "cut" were transferred to other agencies.

To calculate the staff cuts, Clinton officials did not count 800 jobs in the White House Offices of Management and Budget and U.S. Trade Representative, nor departments and agencies that provide administrative support to the White House, nor independent consultants performing various tasks for the White House and other federal agencies.]

February 9, 1993: "[The staff cuts are] both real and symbolic."
White House Chief of Staff Thomas "Mack" McLarty

Whitewater Development Corp., the Clintons' Role in

[In 1993-94, federal investigators examined links between Whitewater Development Corp., an Arkansas real estate venture half-owned by Bill and Hillary Rodham Clinton, and a failed Arkansas S&L, the Madison Guaranty Savings and Loan. There were allegations that James McDougal, Madison's co-owner and a partner in Whitewater, had fraudulently diverted money to Arkansas politicians, including Governor Clinton. It was also learned that a Clinton appointee who had previously done legal work for Madison had run the state agency which regulated Madison.

As a senior partner in Little Rock's Rose law firm, Hillary Rodham Clinton had represented Madison in its effort to stave off bankruptcy, and had received $30,000 in legal fees from the S&L. (In 1989, Madison failed at an estimated cost to taxpayers of $60 million.) In another example of the many potential conflicts-of-interest marking the affair, Webster Hubbell, a senior partner at the Rose firm, later represented the federal government in a suit against Madison's accountants. Hubbell went on to become Bill Clinton's Associate Attorney General.

In July 1993, Vincent Foster, another senior partner at Rose, and Bill Clinton's Deputy White House Counsel, was found dead in a park outside Washington, D.C. Foster was Bill and Hillary Rodham Clinton's lawyer for matters relating to Whitewater. After Foster's death, White House officials removed records pertaining to Whitewater from Foster's office and delivered them to the President and First Lady's personal attorney.]

[A report issued on March 23, 1992 and commissioned by the Clinton campaign stated that the Clintons were inactive, "passive shareholders" in the Whitewater real estate venture.]

November 28, 1988, letter to the head of Whitewater: ". . . I am enclosing a Power of Attorney for you to sign, authorizing me to act on your behalf with respect to matters concerning Whitewater Development Corporation."
Hillary Rodham Clinton

Whitewater Development Corp., and Madison Savings & Loan

October 3, 1991: "When the ripoff artists looted our S&Ls, the President [Bush] was silent. In a Clinton Administration, when people sell their companies and their workers and their country down the river, they'll get called on the carpet."

February 3, 1992: "We fueled the greed of the '80s. We were the self-indulged baby boomers and yuppies. We gave way to the kind of ethos that twisted our politics into instruments of self-serving gratification . . ."
Hillary Rodham Clinton

March 8, 1992: [The following news excerpt appeared about Madison Guaranty Savings & Loan:] "Bill Clinton and his wife were business partners with the owner of a failing savings and loan association that was subject to state regulation early in his tenure as Governor of Arkansas, records show. . . . During this period, the

Clintons appear to have invested little money, so stood to lose little if the [Whitewater real estate venture] failed, but might have cashed in on their 50 percent interest if it had done well . . ."
The New York Times

Whitewater Development Corp., Records Relating to

January 2, 1994: [After mounting public pressure for a thorough investigation of the Whitewater affair, the White House said it had given the Clintons' papers on Whitewater to an ongoing federal inquiry:] ". . . the President has turned over all the [Whitewater] documents to the Justice Department."
White House Senior Adviser George Stephanopoulos

Next day: "It'll take a couple of weeks . . . There's actually quite a bit of documents . . ."
Press Secretary Dee Dee Myers

Whitewater Development Corp., Special Prosecutor or Counsel to Investigate

January 3, 1994: "The Attorney General has repeatedly stated her concern that ousting career professionals from the [Justice Department] investigation [of Whitewater] to replace them with someone of her choosing . . . would be unwise."
Justice Department spokesman Carl Stern

January 5, 1994: "I'm not a lawyer, but in order to trigger a special prosecutor or special counsel there has to be some allegation of wrongdoing."
Press Secretary Dee Dee Myers

January 9, 1994, in denying a need for special prosecutor: "The President and the First Lady have done nothing wrong. They have released every scrap of information that they have about this to a

career [Justice Department] prosecutor . . . who is a Republican, incidentally."
Al Gore

January 12, 1994: "The President has directed me to request you [Attorney General Reno] to appoint as special counsel a respected, impartial, and qualified attorney . . . to conduct an appropriate independent investigation of the Whitewater matter . . ."
White House Counsel Bernard Nussbaum

January 20, 1994: [In reply to Larry King about Robert Fiske's plans for his investigation:] "Whatever he wants to do. I just want to do my job. I don't want to be distracted by this anymore. . . . I didn't do anything wrong. Nobody ever suggested I did."

Whitewater Development Corp., Tax Deductions from

November 20, 1991: "There should be be no more deductibility for irresponsibility."

March 8, 1992: [The following news item detailed some of the Clintons' financial dealings with Whitewater Development Corp.:] ". . . The Clintons improperly deducted at least $5,000 on their personal tax returns in 1984 and 1985 for interest paid on a portion of a least $30,000 in bank loan payments that [the Whitewater real estate venture] made for them . . ."
The New York Times

Wynette, Tammy

January 26, 1992, during the Gennifer Flowers controversy: "I'm not sitting here because I'm some little woman standing by my man, like Tammy Wynette."
Hillary Rodham Clinton

January 27, 1992: "Mrs. Clinton, you have offended every woman and man who love that song ["Stand by Your Man"] . . . I believe you have offended every true country music fan and every person who has 'made it on their own' with no one to take them to a White House."
Country singer Tammy Wynette

January 28, 1992: "I happen to be a country-western fan. If she [Tammy Wynette] feels like I've hurt her feelings, I'm sorry about that."
Hillary Rodham Clinton

A Fanciful Dictionary Entry

Clinton (klin′t'n) (verb). *Pol.* 1.a. To simultaneously take two sides of an issue. 1.b. To take the side of the particular audience you are addressing. 2.a. To say the opposite of what you really mean. 2.b. To verbally engage in deliberate deception: *to do a Clinton.* 3.a. To reverse yourself on an issue. 3.b. To betray a solemn pledge or vow. 4.a. To drone endlessly, with great windiness. 4.b. To deliberately speak in a lengthy and convoluted manner, causing the listener to fall into a stupor. 4.c. To obscure the facts with legalistic mumbo-jumbo. 5. To speak with a hoarse or raspy throat, as if suffering from allergies compounded by verbosity. 6. To vaguely state by avoiding all details. 7. To vaguely state using great detail. 8. To hold endless meetings and seminars that accomplish little or nothing, other than"self-enrichment" for participants. 9. To habitually arrive late for meetings. 10. To recoup, unabashed and unabridged, from a staggering blow; to have resilience. 11. To expend great effort for little or no gain. 12. To consume mass quantities of junk food. 13. *Obscure.* To have an oral fixation. (See Freud.)

—v. *clintoned, clintoning, clintons.* —adj. *clintonized*

Synonyms (verbs): pander, straddle, swerve, fudge, flip-flop, wiggle, waffle, waver, lie, deceive, reverse oneself, fool, beguile, betray, stiff, seduce. (Nouns):"Santa Claus", "pander bear," weathervane, Pinocchio. See"false sincerity", tergiversation, "boy who cried wolf."

[Derivation: *Modern Eng.* Clinton "Blythe," as in"William Jefferson Blythe." See "blithe," (variant "blythe") as in "casual, carefree, blithe use of the facts."] [*First use:* "He's doing a Clinton."—Dan Quayle, October 13, 1992.

Antonyms: *Hillary,* "to say exactly what is on one's mind":*"don't beat around the Bush; instead, hammer home and Hillary your point of view."* Also *Rodham,* "to verbally savage in a harsh, stinging, brutally direct way": *"She rodhamed the heck out of Tammy Wynette."*

REFERENCE NOTES

Quotations Page

"The President must articulate": Speech at Georgetown University, "A New Covenant for American Security," December 12, 1991, Georgetown University press office, p. 2.

"crisis of meaning": Speech by Hillary Rodham Clinton, April 6, 1993, at Liz Carpenter's Lectureship Series (University of Texas at Austin), The White House, p. 3.

Abortion

"I am opposed to abortion": Quoted in *The Washington Times,* July 24, 1992, p. A5.

"always been pro-choice": Bill Clinton for President Committee, Issue Brief, "Bill Clinton on Women's Issues," June 1992.

" . . . we will support . . .": *Putting People First,* September 1992, Times Books, New York, p. 169.

Abortion, Parental Consent for

" . . . I have also supported": *The Comeback Kid,* Charles F. Allen and Jonathan Portis, 1992, Birch Lane Press Book, Published by Carol Publishing Company, New York, p. 147.

"[We] oppose": *Putting People First,* September 1992, p. 170.

Abortion, Vice-President's Views on

"During my 11 years in Congress": Quoted in *The Washington Times,* April 1, 1993, p. A6, John McCaslin column. Reprinted from *The Washington Times.*

"Oppose any federal attempt": *Putting People First,* September 1992, p. 170.

Art, Prohibitions on Federally Funded

"I'm against it": and "Congress passed": Quoted in *The Washington Times,* April 7, 1993, p. A3.

AT&T, Breakup of

" . . . one of the worst ideas": *Arkansas Gazette,* April 14, 1983, p. 5A.

"I think it worked": Quoted on C-SPAN, July 26, 1992.

Baird, Zoe, Withdrawal of Attorney General Nomination for

"It was fully disclosed": *The New York Times,* January 15, 1993, p. A15.

"[Clinton did] not believe" and "Mr. Clinton still believes" and "With sadness": *The New York Times,* January 22, 1993, p. A1.

Balanced Budget

"[I] would present": CNN, June 4, 1992, quoted in *The Washington Post,* June 5, 1992, p. A12.

"in half": Speech before the Economic Club of Detroit, August 21, 1992, transcript, Economic Club of Detroit, p. 4.

"finally they've [members of Congress] got somebody": *The Washington Times,* August 6, 1993, p. A1.

Balanced Budget in Arkansas

"I have balanced 11": Speech before the Economic Club of Detroit, August 21, 1992, transcript, Economic Club of Detroit, p. 3.

Bosnia

"We may have to use military force": *The Los Angeles Times,* August 6, 1992, p. A3.

"problem from hell": Quoted in *The New York Times,* April 8, 1993, p. A1.

"wouldn't rule out": *The Washington Times,* April 17, 1993, p. A1.

"The United States is not" and "I think we should act": *The Washington Times,* April 24, 1993, p. A1.

" . . . we must have": Press conference, April 23, 1993, transcript, *The Washington Post,* April 24, 1993, p. A16.

"fix it position . . .": Quoted in *The Washington Times,* May 19, 1993, p. A9.

"So I can't give" and "I wouldn't rule out": Interview, May 13, 1993, transcript, *The Washington Post*, May 14, 1993, p. A10.

"not vacillating": *The Washington Times*, May 19, 1993, p. A1.

"Our allies decided": *The Washington Times*, June 16, 1993, p. A1.

" . . . my preference was": *The Washington Post*, June 18, 1993, p. A1.

"If the Serbs and the Croats persist": *The Washington Times*, July 9, 1993, p. A10.

"The United States is doing all it can": *The Washington Post*, July 22, 1993, p. A1.

"The United States is committed" and "we should continue to discuss": *The Washington Times*, July 29, 1993, p. A1.

"unwise to depend on any indecision . . .": *The Washington Times*, August 7, 1993, p. A1"; . . . I would remind you": *The Washington Post*, September 3, 1993, p. A1.

"As all of you know": *The Washington Times*, September 9, 1993, p. A3.

"The sharp escalation of shelling": *The Washington Times*, October 19, 1993, p. A10.

"Is Bosnia horrifying": *The Washington Post*, November 13, 1993, p. A6.

"Air power might": *The Washington Times*, January 12, 1994, p. A1.

"[but only] if we": *The Washington Post*, January 12, 1994, p. A1.

Bosnia, Effect of Bombing in
" . . . there is very little" and "There's a lot to commend": Interview, May 13, 1993, transcript, *The Washington Post*, May 14, 1993, p. A10.

Bosnia, "Ethnic Cleansing" in
"Serbian ethnic cleansing" and "little broader framework": Quoted in *The New York Times*, April 8, 1993, p. A1, Thomas L. Friedman article.

Resigned officials: See *The New York Times*, August 24, 1993, p. A7.

BTU Tax (Energy Tax)
"I recommend": State-of-the-Union address, February 17, 1993, transcript, *The New York Times*, February 18, 1993, p. A20.

"It will not be": *The New York Times*, June 9, 1993, p. A1.

"We'll just see": *The Washington Post*, June 9, 1993, p. A1.

" . . . I think the likelihood": *The Washington Post*, July 19, 1993, p. A1.

BTU Tax, Reaction to Reversal of Position on
"the President walked away" and " . . . we've been left hanging": *The Washington Post*, June 11, 1993, p. A1.

Campaign Finance Reform
"First the plan will impose strict . . .": Statement on campaign finance reform, May 7, 1993, The White House, p. 4.

Catholic Church
"The first 400 . . .": *The Washington Times*, September 4, 1993, p. A4, and *The Washington Times*, September 7, 1993, p. E3, Robert George column. Reprinted from *The Washington Times*.

" . . . I enrolled": Speech at University of Notre Dame, September 11, 1992, remarks prepared for delivery, p. 2.

Children, Government Role in Raising
"[G]overnments don't raise": July 16, 1992, presidential nomination acceptance speech, transcript, *The New York Times*, July 17, 1992, p. A14.

"Create a . . .": *Putting People First*, September 1992, p. 48.

"too much responsibility on the mother": *The Comeback Kid*, Charles F. Allen and Jonathan Portis, 1992, p. 212.

China, Sending Envoys to
"ambivalence about supporting democracy": *The Washington Times*, October 2, 1992, p. A4.

"Mr. Bush sent": First presidential debate, October 11, 1992, transcript, *The Washington Post*, October 12, 1992, p. A16.

"You cannot preach": *The Washington Post*, October 21, 1993, p. A28.

Civil Rights, Setting Personal Example for
"across a racial divide": Announcement speech for president, October 3, 1991, transcript, *Arkansas Gazette*, October 4, 1991, p. 12A.

Officials: See *The Washington Post*, August 15, 1993, p. A20.

" . . . [we] must now accept": vice-presidential nomination acceptance speech, transcript, *The Los Angeles Times,* July 17, 1992, p. A11.

Civil Rights Laws in Arkansas and the United States
Arkansas' lack of civil rights laws: *The New York Times,* September 28, 1992, p. A12;-"Support strong and effective enforcement": *Putting People First,* September 1992, p. 64.

Clinton, Bill, Foreign Leaders' Praise For
Hussein: *The Washington Post,* February 15, 1993, p. A29.
Jaruzelski: *The New York Times,* March 4, 1993, p. A1.
Castro: *The Washington Post,* July 31, 1993, p. A18.
Gadhafi: *The Washington Times,* July 6, 1993, p. A1.

Clinton, Bill, Friends of Bill on
Kerrey: *The Washington Times,* February 7, 1992, p. A3.
Tsongas: *The New York Times,* March 7, 1992, p. 11.
"pander bear": See *The New York Times,* March 7, 1992, p. 11.
Moynihan: *The Washington Post,* January 15, 1993, p. A15.
Kennedy: *The Washington Post,* May 14, 1993, p. B1.
Begala: Quoted in *The Washington Times,* May 14, 1993, p. A6, John McCaslin column. Reprinted from *The Washington Times.*
Guinier: Quoted in *The Washington Times,* June 6, 1993, p. A4.
Mfume: Quoted in *The Washington Times,* June 17, 1993, p. A6, John McCaslin column. Reprinted from *The Washington Times.*
"How do I say this": *The Washington Times,* July 18, 1993, p. A4.

Clinton, Bill , White House Counselor David Gergen on
"from poor to perilous" and "good, strong leadership": *The Washington Post,* May 31, 1993, p. A4.

Clinton, Bill, Former Surgeon General C. Everett Koop and
"Now, nobody has": Speech to Congress on health care, September 22, 1993, transcript, *The New York Times,* September 23, 1993, p. A24.
"I'm telling you": *The Washington Times,* November 16, 1992, p. A7.

Commerce Secretary, Foreign Lobbyists and the
"In a Clinton Administration": Speech before the Economic Club of Detroit, August 21, 1992, transcript, Economic Club of Detroit, p. 9.
Work for Duvalier: See *Newsweek,* October 25, 1993, p. 26, and *The Washington Post,* January 16, 1993, p. A1.
"Mr. Brown has never had" and "they did not discuss money": *The Washington Times,* September 29, 1993, p. A3.

Commercial Mining on Park Land in Arkansas
"Governor Bill Clinton has signed legislation": *Arkansas Gazette,* April 9, 1987, p. 2B.
"I've never supported commercial mining": *Arkansas Gazette,* June 27, 1990, p. 6B.

Condom Ads
"I've been naked": *The Washington Times,* January 5, 1994, p. A1.
"We do not feel": *The Washington Times,* January 8, 1994, p. A5.

Credibility, Statements on
"I'm Bill Clinton": *The Washington Times,* January 16, 1993, p. A1.
"bully pulpit into a pulpit of bull": *The Los Angeles Times,* May 22, 1992, p. A22.
"No wonder Americans hate politics": Speech before the Economic Club of Detroit, August 21, 1992, transcript, Economic Club of Detroit, p. 2.
" . . . the most important thing": Press conference, June 17, 1993, transcript, *The Washington Post,* June 18, 1993, p. A10.
"A lesson": *The Washington Times,* December 23, 1993, p. A3.

Cuomo, Mario
Taped remarks: *The Washington Times,* January 28, 1992, p. A6.
"I meant simply to imply . . .": *Arkansas Democrat-Gazette,* January 29, 1992, p. 12A and *The Washington Times,* February 1, 1992, p. B1;-"I think Governor Cuomo": MTV, June 16, 1992.

Day Person vs. Night Person
"A little of both": CBS News, quoted in *The Washington Post*, April 14, 1993, p. A1.

Death Penalty Law, Credit Claimed For Passing
"Gov. Bill Clinton has passed" and ". . . legislation that specifically": *Arkansas Gazette*, April 8, 1990, p. 1A.

Decisiveness
"The American people would think I was foolish": *The Washington Post*, January 15, 1993, p. A1.

"There is no wavering": Press conference, June 15, 1993, transcript, *The Washington Post*, June 16, 1993, p. A14.

"I think in a way": *The Washington Post*, November 9, 1993, p. A1.

Defense Cuts and Deficit Reduction
"reducing our deficit": *Putting People First*, September 1992, p. 133.

"dollar for dollar": *Putting People First*, September 1992, p. 76.

Deficit, Estimating the
"When I began": Interview of June 23, 1992, *Business Week*, July 6, 1992, p. 28.

"I can't": Address on the economy, February 15, 1993, transcript, *The New York Times*, February 16, 1993, p. A14.

Deficit figure: *A Vision of Change For America*, February 17, 1993, The White House, p. 145.

Deficit, Reducing the Size of the
"Never again": *Putting People First*, September 1992, p. 8.

Figures on accumulated deficits: *The Washington Post*, August 4, 1993, p. A11.

"Deficit Reduction" Accord, Follow-up to
"We're just getting": *The Washington Times*, August 3, 1993, p. A4.

Spending increases: See for example *The Washington Post*, October 5, 1993, p. A12, *The Washington Post*, September 23, 1993, p. A23, *The Washington Times*, September 22, 1993, p. A1, and *The Washington Times*, November 16, 1993, p. A10.

Demonstrations, Organizing Anti-Vietnam War
"I went to Washington": Letter from Bill Clinton to director of University of Arkansas ROTC program, December 3, 1969, transcript, *The Washington Times*, September 17, 1992, p. A8 (Associated Press).

"The stories you mentioned": Quoted in *The Washington Times*, October 29, 1992, p. G3, Paul Greenberg column; "He [Clinton] was one": *The Washington Times*, September 18, 1992, p. A1.

Demonstrators, Meeting Overseas With Anti-Vietnam-War
Question-and-answer session and "We went to various places": Quoted in *The Washington Times*, October 8, 1992, p. A1.

"Diversity"
"look like America": Final presidential debate, October 19, 1992, transcript, *The New York Times*, October 20, 1992, p. A20.

Lawyer's tally: *The Washington Post*, January 14, 1993, p. A29, George Will column.

Millionaires: See for example *The Washington Times*, January 27, 1993, p. A3.

Draft, Evading the Vietnam
"not just for saving me from the draft": Letter to director of University of Arkansas ROTC, December 3, 1969, transcript, *The Washington Times*, September 17, 1992, p. A8 (Associated Press).

"I put myself in a position to be drafted": Quoted in *The Washington Times*, February 16, 1992, p. B1, Paul Greenberg column.

"We must make good": Speech at Georgetown University, "The New Covenant: Responsibility and Rebuilding the American Community," October 23, 1991, Georgetown University press office, p. 3.

"I didn't go back through": *The Washington Times*, September 16, 1992, p. A4.

"it could take a political toll": *The Washington Times*, September 16, 1992, p. A1.

"You drew a conclusion": Quoted in *The Washington Times*, October 7, 1992, p. A4, Wesley Pruden column. Reprinted from *The Washington Times*.

Draft Evasion and the Arkansas Senator

"I am positive I never asked anyone": *The Washington Times,* October 8, 1992, p. G4, Donald Lambro column. Reprinted from *The Washington Times.*

"Governor Clinton has no specific recollection" and "[Governor Clinton] talked": *The New York Times,* September 19, 1992, p. 1.

Draft Evasion and Family Influence

"all news to me": Quoted in *The Washington Times,* September 5, 1992, p. A1.

"I did not know": *The Washington Times,* September 5, 1992, p. A1.

"He [Clinton] never asked": *The Washington Times,* September 20, 1992, p. A1.

"Since he's running": *The Washington Times,* October 8, 1992, p. A1.

"If I had it [the draft] to do over": Final presidential debate, October 19, 1992, transcript, *The New York Times,* October 20, 1992, p. A20.

Draft Evasion and the ROTC Letter

All quotations from letter to director of University of Arkansas ROTC program, December 3, 1969, transcript, *The Washington Times,* September 17, 1992, p. A8 (Associated Press).

Draft Notice, Receipt of a

" . . . I told the [draft board]": Quoted in *The Washington Times,* October 8, 1992, p. G4, Donald Lambro column. Reprinted from *The Washington Times;-*" . . . in 1969, while studying at Oxford": August 25, 1992, speech before the American Legion, transcript, p. 2. See *The Washington Times,* October 8, 1992, p. G4, Donald Lambro column.

Drug Treatment Programs

"Our aim": "Weekly Compilation of Presidential Documents," Office of the Federal Register, July 5, 1993, p. 1213.

"Frankly" and "That's something": *The Washington Post,* July 2, 1993, p. A9.

"not what we wanted to see happen": *The Washington Post,* July 8, 1993, p. A6.

Drugs, Legalizing

" . . . I have a brother": First presidential debate, October 11, 1992, transcript, *The Washington Post,* October 12, 1992, p. A16.

"And I do feel" and "She [Elders] is not speaking": *The Washington Post,* December 8, 1993, p. A3.

Drugs, War on

"I will": July 16, 1992, presidential nomination acceptance speech, transcript, *The New York Times,* July 17, 1992, p. A14.

"we would provide them [prostitutes] Norplant": Quoted in *The Washington Times,* June 27, 1993, p. A1.

Education Spending Under George Bush

"not accurate . . . not fair": *Arkansas Gazette,* February 27, 1990, p. 1A.

"For four years": *Putting People First,* September 1992, p. 84.

Elderly, Views on Earnings of the

"Lift the Social Security earnings test limitation": *Putting People First,* September 1992, p. 141.

85 percent tax: *The New York Times,* August 8, 1993, p. 22.

Environment, Foreign Aid and the

Quayle/Gore exchange: October 13, 1992, vice-presidential debate, transcript, *The Washington Post,* October 14, 1992, p. A15.

"annual U.S. expenditures": *Earth in the Balance: Ecology and the Human Spirit,* Houghton Mifflin, Boston, 1992, p. 304.

Environment, Gore Family and Garbage Dump

"The task of saving": Al Gore, July 16, 1992, vice-presidential nomination acceptance speech, transcript, *The Los Angeles Times,* July 17, 1992, p. A11.

"Our [family] farm" : *Earth in the Balance: Ecology and the Human Spirit,* p 3.

October 1992 report and ". . . may be ugly": *The Washington Times,* October 29, 1992, p. A1.

Environmental Record

"To many Arkansas environmentalists": League of Conservation Voters, 1992 Presidential Profiles (Bill Clinton).

"Gov. Clinton has helped": *Putting People First,* September 1992, p. 180.

Europe and Japan, Importance to the United States of
"[Japan is]": *The Washington Post,* February 13, 1993, p. A25.
"And you": *The Washington Post,* January 10, 1994, p. A11.

Executive Salaries
The Washington Times, January 22, 1992, p. F3, Paul Greenberg column.

Extramarital Affairs, Allegations by Arkansas State Troopers Concerning
"ridiculous": *The Washington Post,* December 23, 1993, p. A1.
Presidential Press Conference, *The Washington Times,* December 23, 1993, p. A1.
"[Sex] is not . . .": *The Washington Times,* February 4, 1994, p. A9.

Farm Research, Reducing Bloat in
Tabular data: *A Vision of Change for America,* February 17, 1993, The White House, pp. 122, 133.

First Hundred Days
"I'll have": ABC News, *Good Morning America,* June 23, 1992, quoted in *The Washington Times,*
    January 15, 1993, p. A1.
"I do think": Quoted in *The Washington Post,* January 21, 1993, p. A21.
"People of the press": *The Washington Times,* January 12, 1993, p. A1.
"I don't know who led you to believe that": *The Washington Post,* January 15, 1993, p. A1.
" . . . I knew when I got there": Quoted in *The Washington Times,* May 11, 1993, p. A4, Wesley
    Pruden column. Reprinted from *The Washington Times.*

First Lady's Accent
Quoted in *The Comeback Kid,* Charles F. Allen and Jonathan Portis, 1992, p. 216.
"Oh well, we all have": *The Washington Post,* July 12, 1993, p. B1.

First Lady's Name
"It was a personal decision": ABC, *Primetime,* January 30, 1992.
"There is no dress rehearsal": Speech by Hillary Rodham Clinton to Wellesley College, May 29,
    1992, Wellesley College, p. 5.

Flowers, Gennifer
" . . . they've been exposed": *The Washington Times,* January 18, 1992, p. A4.
"You know": CBS, *60 Minutes,* quoted in *The Washington Times,* January 27, 1992, p. A1.

Foreign Intervention, Congressional Approval for Armed
"And of course": *The Washington Times,* September 9, 1993, p. A3.
"I thought I . . .": *The Washington Post,* October 19, 1993, p. A1.

Foster, Vincent, Office Search of Deceased White House Aide
" . . . I think that" and "Following the": *The New York Times,* December 22, 1993, p. A20.

Foster, Vincent, Status of Office Files of Deceased White House Aide
"I think": *The Washington Times,* December 22, 1993, p. A1.
"The President has instructed": *The New York Times,* December 24, 1993, p. A1.

Gasoline Tax
Tax and fee increase: See *The Comeback Kid,* Charles F. Allen and Jonathan Portis, 1992, p. 62.
"people driving pickup trucks": July 16, 1992, presidential nomination acceptance speech, transcipt,
    The New York Times, July 17, 1992, p. A14;
"I haven't signed off yet": Quoted on National Public Radio, June 10, 1993.
"The plan asks": Televised address, transcript, *The Washington Post,* August 4, 1993, p. A10.

Gays in the Military
"repeal the ban on gays and lesbians": *Putting People First,* September 1992, p. 64.
"I've made no decision": *The New York Times,* November 17, 1992, p. A18;
"I have not backed away": *The New York Times,* January 14, 1993, p. A10.
"This is not an area . . .": CBS, "48 Hours," Quoted in *The Washington Post,* March 27, 1993.
"That's sort of my position": Quoted in *The Washington Times,* May 11, 1993, p. A4, Wesley Pruden
    column. Reprinted from *The Washington Times.*
"I support the present code of conduct": *The Washington Times,* May 15, 1993, p. A6.
"My sense is": *The Washington Times,* July 15, 1993, p. A1.
"the presence . . . of persons": *The Washington Post,* October 27, 1993, p. A4.

"Global Warming," Delay and Changes to Plan for Reducing

"[Global warming is] the": *The New Republic,* July 6, 1992, p. 23.

"They embarrassed our nation": Al Gore, July 16, 1992, vice-presidential nomination acceptance speech, excerpts, *The New York Times,* July 17, 1992, p. A15.

Announcement of deadline: *Time,* May 3, 1993, p. 59.

"The delay speaks": *The Washington Post,* August 16, 1993, p. A5.

"Voluntary is not": *The New York Times,* October 20, 1993, p. A20.

"But the magnitude of the threat": *The Climate Change Action Plan,* Bill Clinton and Al Gore, October 1993, p. I.

Golf Handicap

"Well, it's about a 14 . . .": *The Washington Times,* August 31, 1993, p. A6, Mike McCaslin column, quoting article by Mike Barnicle of *The Boston Globe.* Reprinted from *The Washington Times.*

Government Role towards Private Industry

"[I recommend] [t]ax incentives": Al Gore, *Earth in the Balance: Ecology and the Human Spirit,* p 320.

"picking winners": Speech before the Economic Club of Detroit, August 21, 1992, transcript, Economic Club of Detroit, p. 8.

Government Workers, Decreasing the Number of

"This reduction": *From Red Tape to Results: Creating a Government That Works Better & Costs Less* ("reinventing government" report), Vice President Al Gore, September 7, 1993, p. iii.

"I do not know": *The Washington Post,* October 14, 1993, p. A29.

Guinier, Lani: Withdrawal of Nomination for Assistant Attorney General for Civil Rights

"I want to say" and "I would never have appointed": Quoted in *The Washington Times,* June 20, 1993, p. B4, Paul Greenberg column.

"I think that I have to talk . . .": *The New York Times,* June 3, 1993, p. A1.

"It is with deep regret" and "even though" and "Now I want": *The Washington Post,* June 4, 1993, p. A10;

"I love her" and "If she called . . .": Quoted in *The Washington Times,* June 20, 1993, p. B4, Paul Greenberg column.

Guinier, Lani: Followup Selection for Assistant Attorney General for Civil Rights

Payton voting record and "Well, it was": *The Washington Post,* December 18, 1993, p. A1.

"We are going": *The Washington Post,* November 5, 1993, p. A10.

"Sadly": *The Washington Times,* December 18, 1993, p. A1.

" . . . nobody's accused me": "The *Rolling Stone* Interview: President Clinton." By John S. Wenner and William Greider, from *Rolling Stone,* December 9, 1993, p. 42. By Straight Arrow Publishers, Inc., 1993. All Rights Reserved. Reprinted by permission.

Gun Control

"I'm not for gun control": *Arkansas Gazette,* November 2, 1990, p. 9B.

" . . . pass the": "The *Rolling Stone* Interview: President Clinton." By John S. Wenner and William Greider, from *Rolling Stone,* December 9, 1993, p. 45. By Straight Arrow Publishers, Inc., 1993. All Rights Reserved. Reprinted by permission.

"You are going": *The Washington Post,* December 21, 1993, p. A3.

Haircut Costing $200 From Hollywood Hairdresser on Runway of Los Angeles International (LAX) Airport

"According to the information I had" and "It wouldn't necessarily be unusual": *The Washington Times,* May 23, 1993, p. B2, editorial. Reprinted from *The Washington Times.*

"Bill Clinton has challenging hair": *The Washington Post,* May 21, 1993, p. A11.

"We had a good week" and "The president was disappointed in the week": *The Washington Times,* May 25, 1993, p. A1.

"I would never do that": *The Washington Post,* May 28, 1993, p. A14.

Haiti, Remarks on Sending U.S. Troops to

"When lives are on the line": *The Washington Post,* September 28, 1993, p. A1.

Blocked landing: *The Washington Post,* October 13, 1993, p. A1.

" . . . I was not about": Press conference, October 14, 1993, excerpts, *The Washington Times,* October 15, 1993, p. A19.

"[I must make] absolutely clear": *The Washington Post,* October 15, 1993, p. A1.

"We had every reason to think": *The Washington Post,* October 17, 1993, p. A29.

Haiti, Role of U.S. Troops Sent to

"I have no intention" and "This is not": *The Washington Times,* October 13, 1993, p. A1.

Haitian Refugees, Forcible Return of

"I think the President": *Miami Herald,* March 4, 1992, p. 22A.

"The practice of returning" and "I still believe": *The Washington Post,* January 15, 1993, pp. A1, A16.

"believe just exactly": *The Washington Post,* January 15, 1993, p. A1.

"Sometimes people only hear half the message": *The Washington Times,* January 15, 1993, p. A1.

" . . . when I took office": *The Washington Times,* October 15, 1993, p. A19.

"Head Start" Program for Pre-School Children

"We all know": State-of-the-Union speech, February 17, 1993, transcript, *The New York Times,* February 18, 1993, p. A20.

"The well-known formula": *Time,* March 8, 1993, p. 43.

Health Care Budget

"We could cover every American": Speech at Georgetown University, "A New Covenant for Economic Change," November 20, 1991, Georgetown University press office, p. 8.

" . . . $30 billion" and '$100 billion': *The Washington Times,* April 23, 1993, p. C1.

Moynihan quote: *The Washington Post,* September 20, 1993, p. A1.

Health Care Choice

"People don't want": Speech at Georgetown University, "The New Covenant: Responsibility and Rebuilding the American Community," October 23, 1991, Georgetown University press office, p. 4;

Draft recommendations: Quoted in *The Washington Times,* October 27, 1993, p. A21, Morgan Reynolds column.

Health Care, Federal Role in

"We've got to quit": *The New York Times,* September 25, 1992, p. A1.

"I can understand how": *The Washington Post,* June 14, 1993, p. A6.

Health Care Plan, Accurately Predicting Impact of

"There shouldn't be": Quoted in *National Review,* October 18, 1993, p. 22.

" . . . [we used] the most": Quoted in *National Review,* October 18, 1993, p. 22.

" . . . we just don't have": *The Washington Times,* October 12, 1993, p. A5.

Health Care Plan, Percentage of People Paying More Under

"This was the first time"*:* Speech to Congress on health care, September 22, 1993, transcript, *The New York Times,* September 23, 1993, p. A24.

"32 percent": *The Washington Times,* November 2, 1993, p. A3.

" . . . a few people" and "40 percent": *The Washington Post,* October 29, 1993, p. A1.

"One hundred percent": *The Washington Times,* October 29, 1993, p. A4.

"So let's stop": *The Washington Times,* November 2, 1993, p. A3.

"30 percent": *The Washington Times,* November 5, 1993, p. A3.

Health Care Plan, Timetable For

"In the first year": Speech at Georgetown University, "A New Covenant for Economic Change," November 20, 1991, Georgetown University press office, p. 8.

"offer, within the first one hundred days": Town meeting, Jacksonville, FL, September 9, 1992.

"Later this spring": State-of-the-Union speech, February 17, 1993, transcript, *The New York Times,* February 18, 1993, p. A20.

"I personally am quite close": Press conference, June 17, 1993, transcript, *The Washington Post,* June 18, 1993, p. A10.

"exact timing is still under discussion": *The Washington Post,* July 30, 1993, p. A6.

"I think we have a chance to pass something": *Fortune,* August 23, 1993, p. 60.

"We don't have a hard deadline on it": *The Washington Times,* October 13, 1993, p. A20.

"I ask that": Speech on health care, October 27, 1993, transcript, *The Washington Times,* October 28, 1993, p. A14.

"The debate is no longer": *The Washington Times,* October 29, 1993, p. A4.

Health Care Task Force, Closed Meetings of Hillary Rodham Clinton's

"all the players": *Dallas Morning News,* October 7, 1991, p. 19A.

" . . . the court takes no pleasure" and "[The president is] very gratified": *The Washington Post,* March 11, 1993, p. A18, and *The Washington Times, Insight* magazine, April 4, 1993, p. 32.

"The Justice Department feels": *The Washington Post,* March 23, 1993, p. A8.

" . . . I have been deeply moved": Speech to Congress on health care, September 22, 1993, transcript, *The New York Times,* September 23, 1993, p. A24.

"I'd like to think": *Family Circle* magazine, July 21, 1992, p. 44.

Health Care Taxes

"We don't need": Clinton Campaign Issue Brief, 1992.

"payroll tax": August 12, 1992, meeting with newspaper editors, quoted in *The Washington Times,* September 27, 1992, p. A6.

"We haven't proposed": August 25, 1992, PBS, *MacNeil-Lehrer Newshour.*

"I think there is a possibility": *The Washington Times,* February 22, 1993, p. A1.

"no decision has been made": News conference, March 23, 1993, *The Washington Post,* March 24, 1993, p. A16.

"[health care plan is] going": *The Washington Post,* April 15, 1993, p. A1.

"At least at the present": *Fortune,* August 23, 1993, p. 59.

Question-and-answer: *The Washington Times,* September 29, 1993, p. A15.

Hispanic for Supreme Court, Nominating an

"The old adage": *Dallas Morning News,* July 2, 1992, p. 13A.

Short list: See for example *The Washington Post,* June 15, 1993, p. A11.

Hussein, Saddam

" . . . we sent him": Final presidential debate, October 19, 1992, transcript, *The New York Times,* October 20, 1993, p. A20.

"I think . . .": Interview, January 13, 1993, transcript, *The New York Times,* January 14, 1993, p. A10.

Influence Peddling

"For too many Americans": Speech at Georgetown University, "A New Covenant for Economic Change," November 20, 1991, Georgetown University press office, p. 3.

"We're going to take on the lobbyists": *The Washington Times,* February 7, 1993, p. A1.

Congressional Dinner: *The Washington Post,* May 6, 1993, p. A21.

President's Dinner: *The Washington Post,* June 10, 1993, p. A1.

Jackson, Jesse, President's Temper and

"I think the trick": *Time,* December 13, 1993, p. 42.

"It's an outrage . . .": *The Comeback Kid,* Charles F. Allen and Jonathan Portis, 1992, pp. 219-220.

"I didn't fly off the handle": *Arkansas Democrat-Gazette,* February 28, 1992, p. 12A.

Japan Summit, Results From

"What distinguishes this summit": *The Washington Post,* July 8, 1993, p. A1.

"We should have no illusions": *The Washington Post,* July 10, 1993, p. A1.

Job Discrimination by Race or Gender

"[We oppose] . . .": *Putting People First,* September 1992, pp. 64, 171.

"I believe": News conference, April 23, 1993, transcript, *The Washington Post,* April 24, 1993, p. A16.

"White House personnel": *The Washington Post,* November 22, 1993, p. A19.

21 of 33: *The Washington Post,* October 29, 1993, p. A25, Al Kamen column.

Job Quotas for Women

"For 12 years": Speech at Georgetown University, "The New Covenant: Responsibility and Rebuilding the American Community," October 23, 1991, Georgetown University press office, p. 8.

"I would not restrict myself": *The Denver Post,* March 1, 1992, p 4A.

"There's no reason": *The Washington Times,* August 25, 1992, p. A4.

"bean counters . . ." and "More than three": *The Washington Times,* December 22, 1992, p. A1.

Jobs Bill, Cost of

"Whether it's $15 billion": *The Washington Post,* January 28, 1993, p. A10.

"It's all in the same range": *The Washington Post,* February 3, 1993, p. A15, Al Kamen column, copyright © 1993. *The Washington Post.* Reprinted with permission.

"in the ballpark" and "Among the figures . . .": *The Washington Times,* February 3, 1993, p. A1.

Jogging Track on White House Lawn
Question-and-answer session: *The Washington Post,* February 18, 1993, p. C1, Lloyd Grove article. © 1993 The Washington Post, reprinted with permission.

Junk Food, Bill Clinton and
"[Children] might have special standing": From *Children's Rights: Contemporary Perspectives,* quoted in National Review, May 11, 1992, p. 35.

"I don't necessarily consider McDonald's": *The Washington Post,* April 29, 1993, p. D3.

"People say to me": *The Washington Post,* Novermber 11, 1993, p. C3, Lois Romano, "Reliable Source" column.

Jury Selection, Fairness in
"It is a sad day": Quoted in *The Washington Times,* February 26, 1993, p. F1, Bruce Fein column. Reprinted from *The Washington Times.*

"Although the [Justice Department] . . .": *The Washington Times,* February 24, 1993, p. A1.

Kosher Kitchen in the White House
"[I would] keep a glatt kosher kitchen": *Washington Jewish Times,* April 3, 1992, p. 17.

"We don't serve kosher meals": Telephone conversation between author and employee of White House kitchen, August 12, 1993.

Labor Unions
" . . . the vociferous, organized opposition . . .": *The Washington Times,* November 8, 1993, p. A1.

Lieutenant Governor's Race in Arkansas
"It was not" and "There was a very hostile climate": *The Washington Times,* July 29, 1993, p. A4.

Limbaugh, Rush, Armed Forces Broadcast of
"The Rush Limbaugh [radio] show": *The Washington Times,* November 29, 1993, p. A1.

"We'll broadcast": *The Washington Times,* December 3, 1993, p. A4.

Line Item Veto for the Federal Budget
"strongly in favor": Press release, June 1992.

"[House Speaker Tom Foley] made an intriguing suggestion": *The New York Times,* November 17, 1992, p. A18.

Lobbying, "Revolving Door" Between Government Service and
"I think we should make it . . .": *The Washington Post,* December 12, 1993, p. A1.

"The American people have a right to know": *A Vision of Change For America,* February 17, 1993, The White House, p. 114.

"I don't think we should": *The Washington Post,* December 9, 1993, p. A4.

"There is a standard": *The Washington Times,* December 20, 1993, p. A20, Paul Greenberg column.

"So I also must now call": State-of-the-Union speech, January 25, 1994, transcript, *The Washington Post,* January 26, 1994, p. A12.

Lobbyists
"The last 12 years": *Putting People First,* September 1992, p. 24.

"Many have already lined": Address on the economy, February 15, 1993, *The New York Times,* February 16, 1993, p. A14.

Los Angeles Riots, Blame For
"[Republicans supported] more than a decade": *Arkansas Democrat-Gazette,* May 1, 1992, p. 14A.

"I don't think today is the day": *The Los Angeles Times,* May 2, 1992, p. A12.

Los Angeles Riots, Responsibility for Looting During
"I would show no sympathy": *Arkansas Democrat-Gazette,* May 2, 1992, p. 1A.

"Oh, to be sure, it was heartbreaking": *The San Francisco Chronicle,* May 11, 1992, p. A2.

Marijuana, Smoking
"[I've never] broken any drug law": *Arkansas Gazette,* July 24, 1991, p. 8B.

"never broken a state law . . ." and "Nobody's ever asked me": *The New York Times,* March 30, 1992, p. A15.

Meaning, Communication, and the First Lady

"We have to first create": Quoted in *The Washington Times,* June 4, 1993, p. F4, Paul Greenberg column.

"I hope one day": *The New York Times Magazine,* May 23, 1993, p. 22;

"one of the things": *The Washington Post,* August 1, 1993, p. A1.

Media, Attitude on the

"Some of them . . .": "*The Rolling Stone* Interview: President Clinton." By John S. Wenner and William Greider, from *Rolling Stone,* December 9, 1993, pp. 42, 43, 81. By Straight Arrow Publishers, Inc., 1993. All Rights Reserved. Reprinted by permission.

Medical Records, Releasing the President's

"We feel that this is a privacy issue": *The New York Times,* October 10, 1992, p. A1.

Dismissal of physician: *Time,* February 8, 1993, p. 18.

Medicare

" . . . there's about $60 billion": Speech to Business Roundtable, June 9, 1993, The White House, p. 5.

" . . . we must protect older Americans": Nationally televised address, August 3, 1993, transcript, *The Washington Post,* August 4, 1993, p. A10.

Middle-Class Tax Cut

" . . . starts with a tax cut" and "I'm going to have to at least modify" and "The press and my political opponents": Quoted in *The Washington Times,* January 16, 1993, p. A8.

"I'm not going to raise taxes on the middle class": Third presidential debate, October 19, 1992, transcript, *The New York Times,* October 20, 1992, p. A20.

Various proposals: See *Putting People First,* September 1992, p. 15, and *The Washington Post,* January 14, 1993, p. 29, George Will column.

"I never did meet any voter": Quoted in *The Washington Times,* January 16, 1993, p. A8.

"To middle-class Americans . . .": State-of-the-Union speech, February 17, 1993, transcript, *The New York Times,* February 18, 1993, p. A20.

" . . . give me four years": *USA Today,* May 18, 1993, p. 4A.

"I pledged . . . to seek": *The Washington Times,* August 1, 1993, p. A1.

Mileage Standards For Cars

"We'll seek to raise": "Earth Day" remarks at Drexel University, April 22, 1992.

"I don't think it's fair": *The Washington Times,* September 27, 1992, p. A6. See *The Washington Post,* August 26, 1992, p. A23, Rowland Evans and Robert Novak column, and *Detroit Free Press,* August 22, 1992, p. 9A.

Millionaires Tax (A Million Ain't Worth What It Used to Be)

"[Impose] surtax": *Putting People First,* September 1992, p. 31.

"10 percent surtax": State-of-the-Union address, February 17, 1993, transcript, *The New York Times,* February 18, 1993, p. A20.

Congressional passage: *The New York Times,* August 8, 1993, p. 22.

"Murphy Brown" Show, Dan Quayle's Remarks About

"just another 'lifestyle choice'": *The Los Angeles Times,* May 20, 1992, p. A1.

"The world is": *The Los Angeles Times,* May 20, 1992, p. A1.

"there's a lot of violence" and "I agree that": *Arkansas Democrat-Gazette,* May 21, 1992, p. 13A.

"it [Quayle's statement] ignores" and "Like any parent": *The Los Angeles Times,* May 22, 1992, p. A22;

" . . . the debate over": Speech by Hillary Rodham Clinton, April 6, 1993, at Liz Carpenter's Lectureship Series (University of Texas at Austin), The White House, p. 6.

"I read his whole speech": *The Washington Times,* December 4, 1993, p. A1.

NAFTA (North American Free Trade Agreement)

"And I supported": Speech at Georgetown University, "A New Covenant for American Security," December 12, 1991, Georgetown University press office, p. 2.

"I'm reviewing it": Remarks during appearance at Detroit Economic Club, August 21, 1992.

"You know" and "Neither I" and "I am the one": Final presidential debate, October 19, 1992, transcript, *The New York Times,* October 20, 1992, p. A20.

"we all recognize the important stakes": *The New York Times,* September 15, 1993, p. A1.

"[The treaty is a] symbol": *The Washington Post,* October 5, 1993, p. A13.

"like flies on a June bug": *The New York Times,* November 2, 1993, p. B9.

NAFTA, Deals Made to Win Passage of

"The people that I've talked to": *The Washington Times,* November 17, 1993, p. A1.

Deals: See for example *The Washington Post,* November 1, 1993, p. A7 and November 18, 1993, p. A1, and *The Washington Times,* November 16, 1993, p. A15, James Sheehan column and December 26, 1993, p. C2, Charles Lewis column.

"Nannygate" (Non-Payment of Social Security Taxes For Household Help)

" . . . you have to": Second presidential debate, October 15, 1992, transcript, *The New York Times,* October 16, 1993, p. A11.

Chater and Thompson: *The Washington Post,* August 4, 1993, p. A3.

Baird: *The New York Times,* January 22, 1993, p. A1.

Wood: *The Washington Post,* February 6, 1993, p. A1.

Brown and Pena: *The Washington Post,* June 14, 1993, p. A1.

Inman: *The New York Times,* December 21, 1993, p. A1.

Bill and Hillary Rodham Clinton: *The American Spectator,* August 1993, p. 21–22.

"Nannygate" and Standards in Federal Hiring

"[I support] efforts": *Putting People First,* September 1992, p. 171.

National Police Force

"Transfer law": *From Red Tape to Results: Creating a Government That Works Better & Costs Less* ("reinventing government" report), Vice President Al Gore, September 7, 1993, p. 102.

" . . . just to reorganize something": *The Washington Post,* September 9, 1993, p. A7.

"Clearly, the vision": Hearing on the Federal Bureau of Investigation and the Drug Enforcement Administration, Committee on the Judiciary, House of Representatives, statement of Deputy Attorney General Philip Heymann, September 29, 1993, p. 9.

" . . . a printing error": *The Washington Times,* October 22, 1993, p. A6.

National Service, Financing College through

"We offer a solution": *The Washington Times,* October 7, 1992, p. A4.

". . . small pilot program": *The Washington Post,* February 4, 1993, p. A1.

Senate bill: *The Washington Post,* September 9, 1993, p. A1.

"New Covenant"

Speech at Georgetown University, "A New Covenant for Economic Change," November 20, 1991, Georgetown University press office, p. 3.

Nominees to High Office, Speed in Confirming

" . . . I was the first" and Nixon/Kennedy facts: *The Washington Times,* May 28, 1993, p. A6, John McCaslin column. Reprinted from *The Washington Times.*

North Korea, the Nuclear Bomb and

"The ball is now in North": *The Washington Times,* November 4, 1993, p. A13.

"Clearly, the ball is": *The Washington Times,* December 8, 1993, p. A3.

"North Korea cannot": *The Washington Times,* November 8, 1993, p. A1.

" . . . [the North Koreans] might": *The Washington Post,* December 13, 1993, p. A13 and *The Washington Times,* December 13, 1993, p. A1.

"We in no sense": *The Washington Times,* December 22, 1993, p. A12.

"We're just going": *The Washington Times,* December 5, 1993, p. A4.

Nuclear Bomb Materials, Banning Production of

"Growing global stockpiles": Speech to the U.N., September 27, 1993, excerpts, *The Washington Times,* September 28, 1993, p. A14.

"I have not": *The Washington Post,* November 12, 1993, p. A10.

Ozone Depletion

". . . yet even now": *Earth in the Balance,* p. 292.

DuPont request and "Given the relatively small change": *The Washington Post,* December 18, 1993, p. C1.

Pay Raise as Arkansas Governor

"I've never had a pay raise": Quoted in *The Washington Times,* January 22, 1992, p. F3, Paul Greenberg column.

Pay Raise For Congress

"For 12 years": Clinton campaign commercial, January 16, 1992, quoted in *The Boston Globe*, January 24, 1992, p. 8.

"'. . . personally told me'": *The Boston Globe*, January 24, 1992, p. 8.

Perks and Privileges

Poultry business and trip data, *The Washington Post*, March 22, 1992, p. A1.

"The privilege of public service": *Putting People First*, September 1992, p. 25.

Persian Gulf War, Congressional Vote on

"I agree with the arguments": *Pine Bluff Commercial* (Arkansas), January 15, 1991, quoted in *The Washington Times*, September 27, 1992, p. A6.

"I personally don't think": Quoted in *Time*, April 20, 1992, p. 44.

"I guess I": *The New York Times*, October 4, 1992, p. A1.

"early and unambiguous": Terry Eastland column in *The Washington Times*, August 12, 1992, p. G1.

Personnel Files, Rifling of

"I just want you to know": Quoted in *The Washington Times*, September 3, 1993, p. A1.

"We haven't responded": *The Washington Times*, September 10, 1993, p. A1.

Dismissals: *The Washington Times*, November 11, 1993, p. A1.

Police, Adding 100,000

" . . . provide 100,000": Campaign remarks, October 17, 1992, cited in "The Clinton Administration Plan to Expand Community Policing and Reduce Gun Violence," The White House, August 11, 1993, p1; 13,000 figure: See *The Washington Times*, October 12, 1993, p. A15, Morton Kondracke column.

"up to 50,000": *The Washington Post*, October 25, 1993, p. A25.

Political Insider

"I don't know how": Quoted in *The Washington Times*, October 6, 1991, p. B3, Paul Greenberg column.

"Senator Fulbright's administrative assistant": Convocation address at American University, February 26, 1993, p. 1, American University press office.

"Pork Barrel" Programs

"No": News conference, March 23, 1993, *The Washington Post*, March 24, 1993, p. A16.

Instances of pork: See for example *The New York Times*, September 21, 1993, p. A14, *The Wall Street Journal*, February 23, 1993, p. A20, Scott Hodge article, and *The Washington Times*, April 19, 1993, p. E1, Donald Lambro column.

Poverty, Fighting

" . . . support new anti-poverty initiatives": *Putting People First*, September 1992, p. 65.

Welfare hikes: See *The Washington Post*, April 9, 1993, p. A10, *The Washington Post*, August 8, 1993, p. A16, and *The New York Times*, August 8, 1993, p. 22.

Reinventing Government

Gore's Senate record: The National Taxpayers Union, "Congressional Spending Study,"1990, 2nd Session, and 1991, 1st Session.

Appointment: *From Red Tape to Results: Creating a Government That Works Better & Costs Less* and "reinventing government" report, Vice President Al Gore, September 7, 1993, p. 1.

"I thank the": "Weekly Compilation of Presidential Documents," Office of the Federal Register, March 8, 1993, p. 350.

$108 billion: *From Red Tape to Results,* (see above), p.iii.

$42 billion and $22 billion: *The Washington Post*, October 15, 1993, p. A23.

$305 million: *The Washington Post*, November 17, 1993, p. A21.

"Public confidence": *From Red Tape to Results: Creating a Government That Works Better & Costs Less* ("reinventing government" report), Vice President Al Gore, September 7, 1993, p. 1.

Reinventing Government, Report on

"Here's a sad story": *From Red Tape to Results: Creating a Government That Works Better & Costs Less* and "reinventing government" report, Vice President Al Gore, September 7, 1993, p. 56.

High printing costs: *The Washington Post*, October 1, 1993, p. G1.

Russia's Election, Reaction to Strong Showing by Radicals in

"By approving": *The New York Times*, December 14, 1993, p. A16.

"We would be foolish": *The Washington Times,* January 7, 1994, p. A12.

Savings and Loan, Madison, Role of Hillary Rodham Clinton in
Denials and "limited work": *The Washington Times,* March 20, 1992, p. A1, Jerry Seper article.

School Choice
"I am fascinated": Letter to Wisconsin state representative Polly Williams, October 18, 1990. See *The Washington Times,* January 14, 1993, p. G3, Donald Lambro column.

"We shouldn't give": Address before the National Education Association, July 7, 1992, Federal Information Systems Corporation, p. 3.

School Chosen for Chelsea Clinton
"always will be": *Arkansas Gazette,* April 15, 1990, p. 1A.

"There are great public schools": Second presidential debate, October 15, 1992, transcript, *The New York Times,* October 16, 1992, p. A11.

"not a rejection . . .": Quoted in *The Washington Times,* January 6, 1993, p. A4, Wesley Pruden column. Reprinted from *The Washington Times.* See also *City Paper,* Washington, DC, July 16, 1993, p. 19.

" . . . Governor Clinton supports": *The New York Times,* January 6, 1993, p. A1.

Scratch on President's Chin
"cut himself shaving" and "playing with Chelsea": *The Washington Times,* April 28, 1993, p. E1.

Secretary of State, Resting Habits of the
"Work" and "He was deep": *The Washington Post,* January 10, 1994, p. A11.

Segregated Country Club, Playing Golf at
"A guy asked me . . .": *The New York Times,* March 21, 1992, p. 8.

Serving Out Term as Governor
"it's a bogus issue": *Arkansas Gazette,* April 11, 1990, p. 14B.

"[T]oday I am": Announcement speech for president, October 3, 1991, transcript, *Arkansas Gazette,* October 4, 1991, p. 12A.

Sesame Street (Watching One's Peas and Cues)
"Hardly anyone": *The Washington Times,* October 15, 1993, p. A8;

"Mrs. Clinton is a pea lover": *The Washington Times,* October 16, 1993, p. A4 (Associated Press).

Sexual Restraint
"We taught them what to do": *Evening Times* (West Memphis, Arkansas), March 4, 1992, quoted in *The Washington Times,* June 27, 1993, p. A1.

"The only thing that works": *The Washington Post,* July 24, 1993, p. A8.

"[America is] a repressed": *The Washington Times,* October 22, 1993, p. A1.

"Abstinence is the surest prevention": *The Washington Times,* October 22, 1993, p. A1.

" . . . sex is a good": *The Washington Times,* November 10, 1993, p. A3.

Small Business
"Most new jobs": Speech at Georgetown University, "A New Covenant for Economic Change," November 20, 1991, Georgetown University press office, p. 10.

"every undercapitalized entrepeneur": *The Wall Street Journal,* September 24, 1993, p. A10.

Social Security
Cost-of-living cuts: *Arkansas Gazette,* February 26, 1986, p. 3A.

"We're not going to fool around with Social Security" and "[A cut in Social Security payments]": *The Washington Post,* January 29, 1993, p. A9, and The United Seniors Association.

"[T]he [budget] plan does ask": State-of-the-Union speech, February 17, 1993, transcript, *The New York Times,* February 18, 1993, p. A20.

Somali Warlord Mohamed Aidid
"The purpose of the operation": Quoted in *The Washington Times,* October 21, 1993, p. A20.

"We never went there": Quoted in *The Washington Times,* October 7, 1993, p. A11, and October 21, 1993, p. A20.

"We're not going to tolerate": *The Washington Post,* October 9, 1993, p. A1.

"And, of course": NBC, *Today,* October 8, 1993, quoted in *The Washington Times,* October 9, 1993, p. A1;

"[the U.S. envoy to": *The Washington Post,* October 17, 1993, p. C1, Lloyd Grove article.
" . . . there must be some resolution": News conference, October 14, 1993, excerpts, *The Washington Times,* October 15, 1993, p. A19.
"Everyone thought": *The Washington Post,* December 7, 1993, p. A19.

Somalia, U.S. Troops in
"I agree we cannot commit ground forces": First presidential debate, October 11, 1992, transcript, *The New York Times,* October 12, 1992, p. A14.
"[Our] goal [is] . . .": *The Washington Post,* August 11, 1993, p. A1.
"We have the troops there" and "Our position is not well enough formed . . .": *The Washington Times,* September 18, 1993, p. A1.
"The country can basically": *The Washington Times,* September 29, 1993, p. A1.
"And all around the world": Speech on Somalia, October 7, 1993, transcript, *The Washington Post,* October 8, 1993, p. A21.

South Africa, Ownership of Diamond Stocks in
" . . . all she": *The Washington Times,* July 9, 1992, p. A1.
"I wasn't aware of it . . .": *The Washington Times,* July 14, 1992, p. A7.

Special Interests
"We will eliminate taxpayer subsidies for narrow special interests": *Putting People First,* September 1992, p. 25.
Programs: See for example The Washington Post, September 1, 1993, p. A23, Robert J. Samuelson column.

Spelling, Skill in
" . . . *establishe* a bipartisan": From transmittal memo, Bill Clinton, April 19, 1993. Quoted in *The Washington Times,* September 9, 1993, p. A6, John McCaslin column. Reprinted from *The Washington Times.*
"Don't have to be": *The Washington Post,* September 9, 1993, p. A19.
"Yitzhak Rabin": *The Washington Post,* September 24, 1993, p. C3.

Spending Cuts
" . . . cuts, not gimmicks": State-of-the-Union speech, February 17, 1993, transcript, *The New York Times,* February 18, 1993, p. A20.
List of "budget cuts": *The Washington Post,* March 7, 1993, p. H1, *The Washington Post,* March 18, 1993, p. A25, and *A Vision of Change For America,* February 17, 1993, The White House, p. 124;
"You must wonder": Nationally televised address, August 3, 1993, transcript, *The Washington Post,* August 4, 1993, p. A10.
"And I plead guilty": *The Washington Post,* August 10, 1993, p. A4.
" . . . trust deficit": *The Washington Times,* October 15, 1993, p. A13.

Spending Cuts, Pledge for Major Round of
"Additional cuts would drain": The Washington Post, November 11, 1993, p. A21.

Tax Hike in Arkansas, Stance on
Campaign vow and "I don't think anybody knew": *Arkansas Gazette,* January 7, 1987, p. 1A.
Revenue figures: *Arkansas Gazette,* January 21, 1987, p. 1A.

Taxes, General Attitude on
" . . . new maturity": Quoted in *The Washington Times,* April 29, 1991, p. A4, Wesley Pruden column. Reprinted from *The Washington Times.*
"I reject": Speech before the Economic Club of Detroit, August 21, 1992, transcript, Economic Club of Detroit, p. 4.
" . . . more Americans must contribute": Address on the economy, February 15, 1993, transcript, *The New York Times,* February 16, 1993, p. A14.

Taxes, Paying Their Fair Share of
1992 deductions: *The Washington Post,* April 26, 1993, p. E2.
1986 deductions: *The Washington Post,* December 28, 1993, p. C1.

Taxes, Threshold for Increased
"The tax increase": First presidential debate, October 11, 1992, transcript, *The New York Times,* October 12, 1992, p. A14.

"I now believe": *The Washington Times,* January 20, 1993, p. A1.
Groups affected by actual taxes: See *The New York Times,* August 8, 1993, p. 22.

Term Limits on Elected Officials
"The people have enough sense": *Arkansas Gazette,* October 1, 1990, p. 1B.
"I wouldn't rule out": NBC News, *Meet the Press,* January 5, 1992.
"I know they're popular": Second presidential debate, October 15, 1992, transcript, *The New York Times,* October 16, 1992, p. A11.

Thomas, Clarence, Supreme Court Nomination of
"I don't see how . . .": *Arkansas Democrat,* October 13, 1991, p. 1A.
"I'm not a Senator . . .": *Arkansas Democrat,* October 15, 1991, p. 1A.

Toxic Waste
"Too often, on the environment": *The Comeback Kid,* Charles F. Allen and Jonathan Portis, 1992, p. 248.
"Until all questions": Press release, Office of Vice-President-Elect Al Gore, December 7, 1992, from Greenpeace. See *The Washington Post,* June 22, 1993, p. C10, Coleman McCarthy column.
". . . certain legal obligations": Town meeting, March 10, 1993, quotation from Greenpeace.

Travel Office, Dismissal of Workers at White House
Firings and reinstatement: See *The Washington Post,* July 3, 1993, p. A1.
"[We were] striving": *The Washington Post,* May 22, 1993, p. A1.
"[I] had nothing to do with" and "[U]ltimately anything that happens": *The Washington Post,* May 26, 1993, p. A1.
"While all": *White House Travel Office Management Review,* The White House, July 2, 1993, p. 15.

U.N. Control of U.S. Troops
"operational control": *The Washington Post,* September 22, 1993, p. A1.
"[Somalia] would make me more cautious": *The Washington Post,* October 15, 1993, p. A1.
"The [U.N.] force commander": U.S. Army manual FM 100-23, "Peace Options," quoted in *The Washington Times,* December 15, 1993, p. A1.

Value-Added Tax (VAT)
"I do believe . . ." and "there seems to be growing support": *The Wall Street Journal,* February 22, 1993, p. A2.
"It is not something . . .": *The New York Times,* February 20, 1993, p. A1.
"I'm ruling it out . . .": *The Washington Times,* February 20, 1993, p. A1.
"I think the president ruled that out fairly clearly" and "If a decision is made": *The Washington Post,* April 15, 1993, p. A1.
"Certainly" and "I think a VAT": *The New York Times,* April 15, 1993, p. A1.
"I personally don't": *The Washington Times,* April 17, 1993, p. A1.
"we ought to have a debate": *Fortune,* August 23, 1993, p. 59.
"[T]here's only so much change": *The New York Times,* February 20, 1993, p. A10.

Veterans' Benefits
" . . . the IRS' shameful": Speech before the American Legion, August 25, 1992, transcript, p. 7.
Cost-of-living proposals: *The Washington Post,* August 8, 1993, p. A16;

Waco, Texas, Rationale for Final Federal Assault on Branch Davidian Compound in
"We know that David Koresh": News conference, April 23, 1993, transcript, *The Washington Post,* April 24, 1993, p. A16.
" . . . Examinations of the children": *The Washington Post,* April 24, 1993, p. A8.

Waco, Texas, Responsibility for Final Federal Assault on Branch Davidian Compound in
"I knew it . . ." and "of course the . . ." and "I made the decisions" and "But the President is . . .": *The Washington Times,* April 21, 1993, p. A9.
"It's not possible": *The Washington Post,* April 21, 1993, p. A15.

Welfare Benefits, Time Limit on Receipt of
"We'll give them": Speech at Georgetown University, "The New Covenant: Responsibility and Rebuilding the American Community," October 23, 1991, Georgetown University press office, pp. 7;
"I would go": Quoted in *The New York Times,* October 17, 1992, p. 9.

" . . . give people on welfare": A *Vision of Change For America*, February 17, 1993, The White House, p. 60.

"I'm not a believer": *The New York Times*, June 21, 1993, p. A1.

Wisconsin experiment: *The Washington Post*, November 2, 1993, A6.

"I fear that time limits": *The New York Times*, June 21, 1993, p. A1.

Welfare Reform in Arkansas, Record of

"17,000": *The Washington Times*, September 14, 1992, p. A6.

51,000: Calculated from figures in *The Washington Times*, September 14, 1992, p. A6.

"Come on down": July 16, 1992, presidential nomination speech, transcript, *The New York Times*, July 17, 1992, p. A14.

Welfare Reform Program in Arkansas

"[It was rated] one": *The New Republic*, October 12, 1992, p. 10.

White House Staff, Cutting the

"I'm going to get" and "something we're pointing towards": *The Washington Post*, January 13, 1993, A13;

" . . . I cut the White House staff": Address on the economy, February 15, 1993, transcript, *The New York Times*, February 16, 1993, p. A14.

Budget data from *The Washington Post*, February 10, 1993, p. A1 and *The Washington Post*, April 23, 1993, p. A21.

"real and symbolic": *The Washington Post*, February 10, 1993, p. A1.

Whitewater Development Corp., the Clintons' Role in

Whitewater and Madison: See for example *The Washington Times*, November 5, 1993, p. A1, Jerry Seper article, and *The Washington Post*, November 2, 1993, p. A1.

"passive shareholders" and " . . . I am enclosing": *The Washington Times*, November 4, 1993, p. A1, Jerry Seper article.

Whitewater Development Corp., and Madison Savings and Loan

"When the ripoff artists looted": Announcement speech for president, October 3, 1991, transcript, *Arkansas Gazette*, October 4, 1991, p. 12A.

"We fueled the greed": *The Boston Globe*, February 4, 1992, p. 8.

"Bill Clinton and his wife": *The New York Times*, Jeff Gerth article, March 8, 1992, p. 1. Copyright © 1992 by The New York Times Company. Reprinted by permission.

Whitewater Development Corp., Records Relating to

" . . . the President has turned": *The Washington Post*, Janaury 16, 1994, p. A1.

"It'll take": *The Washington Times*, January 4, 1994, p. A1.

Whitewater Development Corp., Special Prosecutor or Counsel to Investigate

"The Attorney General": *The Washington Times*, January 4, 1994, p. A1.

"I'm not a lawyer": *The Washington Times*, January 6, 1994, p. A1.

"The President and": *The Washington Times*, January 10, 1994, p. A1.

"The President has directed": *The Washington Post*, January 13, 1994, p. A1.

"Larry King Live," January 20, 1994.

Whitewater Development Corp., Tax Deductions from

"no more deductibility": Speech at Georgetown University, "A New Covenant for Economic Change," November 20, 1991, Georgetown University press office, p. 10.

"The Clintons improperly deducted": *The New York Times*, March 8, 1992, p. 1. Copyright © 1992 by the New York Times Company. Reprinted by permission.

Wynette, Tammy

"I'm not sitting here": CBS News, *60 Minutes*, January 26, 1992, quoted in *The Comeback Kid*, Charles F. Allen and Jonathan Portis, 1992, p. 192.

"Mrs. Clinton, you": *Arkansas Democrat-Gazette*, January 29, 1992, p. 12A.

"If she [Tammy Wynette] feels": *The Washington Times*, January 29, 1992, p. A1.

THE FINAL WORD

"I have proved one thing, I'm not very slick:
I often say things I shouldn't." [*]

"It's read-my-lips all over again.
Except this time we can read the record." [†]
Bill Clinton

[*] *The Washington Times,* Paul Greenberg Column, April 27, 1992, p. E3.

[†] Speech before the Economic Club of Detroit, August 21, 1992, transcript, Economic Club of Detroit, p. 2.

ABOUT THE AUTHOR

EDWARD P. MOSER is an editor and a senior analyst for a government consulting firm in the Washington D.C. area. A contributor of topical humor to "The Tonight Show," he has published articles in newspapers including *The Washington Post* and *The Philadelphia Inquirer*. A native of the Bronx, Mr. Moser conducted his undergraduate studies at the State University of New York at Albany, and received his M.A. degree in international affairs from George Washington University. He has worked as an editor and writer for the National Academy of Sciences and as a researcher in the Senate of the United States. He is currently working on two new books of political humor and satire.